Poetry!

52 years of performance poetry
(or John Otway ate my curry.)

By Graham A. Rhodes

First published 2019
Internet Kindle Edition 2019
Second edition 2022

Conditions of Sale.

This book is sold subject to the condition that it shall not, by way of trade or otherwise, be lent, re-sold, hired out, or otherwise circulated without the publishers prior consent, in any form of binding or cover other than that in which it is published.

All rights reserved. No part of this publication may be reproduced, stored in a retrieval system, or transmitted, in any form or by any means, electronic, mechanical, photocopying, recording or otherwise, without the prior permission of the publishers and copyright holder.

Front cover photograph (with thanks) –
Copyright Makiko Kato Brookes

POETRY!

CONTENTS

INTRODUCTION
Scarborough 4

CHAPTER 1
Leeds 7

CHAPTER 2
Harrogate 30

CHAPTER 3
London 86

CHAPTER 4
York 141

CHAPTER 5
Scarborough 194

INTRODUCTION
The Stone Roses Bar York 9.45pm 18th October 2019

It's a damp autumn night in York. Outside the wind is blowing up from the river. Inside the place is packed with York's usual Friday night drinkers and revellers. I'm sat in the "backstage" area Yvonne at my side, a pint of Peroni in front of me. The band members of Northern Riots have just completed their sound check that was so good the crowd thought it was their first number and are buzzing for more. Little do they suspect there's a poet going on-stage before the band begin. Six poems and a hand over to the band who will drift on stage and pick up their instruments as I do my set, so when I've finished they are poised, ready with the first chord.

Making sure I have my reading glasses on I pick up my pint and sheaf of poetry and walk to the edge of the stage. Nils the bands singer songwriter is standing there.

"I'm shit scared!" He says.

"So am I." I reply

I always am, always have been. I glance around, Brad the guitarist gives me a nervous smile, and goes back to fiddling with his foot pedals. Luke the bass player gives me a nod. Kris the drummer is standing ready to get in position. He nods and smiles at me as well. Nils gives me a hug and a kiss on the cheek. Placing my poetry on a stool next to me I take a deep pull of the Peroni, and walk out onto the centre of the stage and take the microphone in hand. I look at the audience who are all looking at the stage in anticipation of a band. The last thing they expect is a seventy year old, ranting poet. For God knows how many times in my life I lift the microphone to my mouth.

Oy Oy!...

Oy Oy

Oy Oy you fuckers....

You can be shit faced
Have shit for brains
Shit or get off the pot

Smoke shit
Talk shit
Or even be shit hot

You can throw shit
Give a shit
Or duck when it hits the fan.....

What follows is the 52 year old story of how I got here.

Graham Rhodes - Scarborough 2019

Chapter One – Leeds pre 1970

So where do we begin? At the beginning I suppose. At the very, very beginning, an early summers evening sat on top of the Gentleman's toilets in Manston Park in a suburb of Leeds, smoking an illicit Embassy cigarette. It was 1965, I was fifteen going on sixteen and pissed off. Some of my mates and school acquaintances were further down the park playing football. A couple of others were breaking into the park keepers hut. Another two were in a far corner of the park strumming cheap guitars and learning songs written by Bob Dylan and Donovan.

Like I said I was pissed off. I wasn't that good at football, I had no ambition to be a burglar, and for the life of me I couldn't get my head around music. Oh, don't get me wrong, I liked listening to it. I was following the charts, buying singles and, when I could afford them, albums. I followed trends and bands, read the music papers. I loved music, I just couldn't play it. For the last three or four years my music teacher at school (Temple Moor Grammar, Selby Road, Whitkirk), had attempted to teach me my A's from my G's, first by letting me scrape a bow across the strings of a violin, then by making squawking sounds with a recorder, but finally he had given up and exiled me to the back of the class with a sort of primitive wooden clapper that I jerked up and down, sometimes in time with the music, sometimes not. My voice was awful. I couldn't hold a note. I couldn't even tell one note from another. I was musically blind. Even at that age I knew I wouldn't make it as a musician, which was why I was pissed off. I rather fancied the lifestyle. Well it was certainly more attractive than the career my school careers master had planned out for me. According to him, if I brushed up on my maths, I just might get a job in the drawing office of some local Leeds engineering works. Incidentally, I was also as crap at maths as I was at music so I had my doubts about that. I was good at something though. Two things in fact. I was good at English, and I was good at drawing. I spent as much time as I could in the art room and found I was very good at drawing with a pencil and with pen and ink. What I really wanted was to go to Art College, but my parents were dead set against that. First of all, like the school careers master, they had no idea of the career opportunities that were available in the world of commercial art. Despite Leeds being home to a couple of large printing works and a number of advertising agencies, as far as my school was concerned it was as if commercial art didn't exist. Secondly, and more importantly, to my parents, art colleges were almost representations of the Anti Christ. They were places where communists and anarchists were born. It was the middle of the sixties. Revolution was in the air, politically and socially. The fashions were changing, long hair, hash and purple hearts had come into the vocabulary, rock music was new and challenging the limits of acceptability to the older generation who, because they had won a war, and lived through the austerity of the 50's thought they knew best. I remember my father sneering at the first TV appearance of the Beatles –

"I could put my foot on everyone of them!" he said.

He nearly had a heart attack when he saw The Rolling Stones, and the Empire was officially declared dead when he caught a glimpse of The Pretty Things. My parents didn't want me to be influenced by such things, they didn't want me to grow my hair long, didn't want me to take drugs, and didn't want me to be influenced by socialism or any other radical new thoughts. Life had been made bad enough during my third year when I came home from school wearing a "Ban the Bomb" badge sold to me for three old pence by our French teacher. It was made even worse that Easter when the TV news showed the Aldermaston March and a crowd of ban the bomb protesters being dragged away by the police. One of them was the teacher that had sold me the badge. He never came back to school. That was enough proof for them that I was in danger of being radicalised and therefore they withheld their parental permission for me to go to art school. It took me years to forgave them for that.

Now, without aim or purpose, I lost any interest I had in taking my GCE's, what's the point I thought. For me Art College was sometime in the future. When I left school with my two GCE's (Art and English) I was doomed to five or six years of dead end jobs, the first being in a food wholesaler, working for a firm called Morris and Jones who supplied Mace grocers. My God that was an eye opener. For a start in was deep in darkest Hunslet, the heavy industrial area of Leeds where the dense atmospheric fug was coloured by whatever chemical was being used by Yorkshire Copperworks that particular day. The entire area lay in a dense pool of coloured smoke, noise and escaping fumes and gasses. For miles around the brickwork was black. Even the pigeons and sparrows coughed.

I'd got the job through a connection of my fathers and was taken on as an office junior, working in the complaints department for the princely sum of £5.10 shillings week. God, the place was like a bad "Carry On" movie. Inside the warehouse was a secret area built inside a series of large cardboard boxes that held toilet rolls, where warehouse people would skive off and play cards. The telephonists office was a glorified knocking shop where office workers would snog and grope each other, heavy petting they called it, and it wasn't just the young ones. The older women (at least in their thirties) were having affairs with half of the senior male management. On top of all that a few lorry drivers, together with some warehouse staff plotted with various shop keepers to mis-deliver certain goods, that went "missing", falling off the backs of lorries never to be seen again. It was a bloody mad house.

Lunch times were spent in a small pub, the interior yellowed by years of cigarette smoke. A place where yesterday's cheese sandwiches curled their edges up in disgust at the colour of the pickled eggs, creatively displayed in screw top jars on the bar alongside the full ashtrays and dirty pint glasses.. In summer when the pub door was opened, the entrance was a boiling cauldron of fumes where the cigarette smoke trying to get outside fought with the polluted air trying to get inside. After almost a year I escaped this particular industrial hell by getting a job at W.H. Smith's in Commercial Street in Leeds City centre. In the next couple of years I would be transferred from the shop to the City Station Bookstall, I didn't care, at least I was out of Hunslet.

But I'm getting ahead of myself, back to the roof of gents toilet.

That particular evening I bumped into a young man I knew slightly. His name was Gordon Davison, and he had a small, self-published book under his arm. It was a book of his own poetry, and it gave him more credibility than playing a guitar or playing football, although he was a very good footballer. He was also one of the area's leading mods with his own scooter. Gordon and I became friends and a few years later, in 1971 we were each other's best men at our respective weddings. I watched him and figured that being a poet was cooler than playing either music or football, especially as I could do neither. I failed at learning the violin, and couldn't get even a simple tune out of a recorder. In fact I was so bad at music I was put at the back of the class with a wooden clapper thing that I was supposed to wave up and down in time with the music. I couldn't! I was crap at even that. So forget music I began writing my own poetry. Most of it was in secret and most of it was awful. Sometimes Gordon and I wrote together. We invented a magazine that we wrote but never got around to publishing, or even printing. We called it "Practical Rhino", well we were both heavily influenced by a radio program called "I'm Sorry I'll Read That Again." It starred comedians who would soon hit our television screens as various Monty Pythons and the Goodies. Most of the stuff we wrote was doggerel but one of Gordon's poems has stuck with me all these years. I'm sure he won't mind me popping it in here

My Uncle fought like a lion
In a tiger skin glued to the cat
He said it's better than fighting a rhino
cos they jump on your hat till its flat
Gordon Davison 1968 ish

That was it for the next few years. I taught myself to write, I discovered sex and alcohol, went to pubs, had friendships, girlfriends, left school, got the dead end Hunslet job, worked in W.H. Smiths, discovered Leeds City Centre, listened to a lot of music, went to a lot of gigs, bought a few records, read a lot and wrote. Thank goodness not a lot of that writing still exists today. It was pretentious teenage angst stuff, about love or the bomb or Vietnam. Obviously it was heavily influenced by my reading. I chose wide and, well after all, I did work in a bookshop and took full advantage of the generous W.H. Smith staff discount. I had a book case built in my bedroom to take this influx of reading matter. This puzzled my Grandmother who once commented

"What do you want another book for? You've already got some." I had.

My mother had given me a good grounding in reading matter. I had read (or had read to me) Alice in Wonderland, Wind In The Willows, Winnie the Pooh, various Enid Blyton Nature Lovers Books, a couple of Biggles, the Gerald Durrell series of books, and every year The Eagle Annual. Now I read Penguin Modern Poets, especially number ten, "The Mersey Sound", the volume that contained the work of Roger McGough, Brian Pattern and Adrian Henri. I read the American writers Richard Brautigan and J. D. Salinger, I read "Catch 22", I read science fiction, I read everything I could get my hands on. I discovered small independent poetry magazines. Of course we were now in the period of so called "underground culture" and its attendant magazines/handbooks such as Oz, Friends, International Times (IT) and Rolling Stone who, as well as publishing music reviews of bands that hadn't hit the mainstream alongside political articles, also published poems. None of which were available at W.H. Smiths! I read the American stuff, the Beat poets like Alan Ginsberg, and Ed Saunders. I read Playboy, not for the nude pictures but for the writing. It was due to that magazine that I discovered Shel Silverstein, (before he became famous for writing lyrics for Dr Hook) I also read the more traditional stuff like Longfellow, Coleridge and of course the War Poets. It was among these that I found one of my all time favourite poets, Robert W. Service.

He was the third of ten children born in Preston to a Scottish father, a banker also called Robert. When he was five he was sent back to Scotland to live with his three maiden aunts and is said to have composed his first poem, a grace, on his sixth birthday. When he left school he became a banker like his father but wrote and sold some of his work, and like myself, was educating himself in poetry by reading Keats, Browning, Tennyson and Thackeray, whom I admit I have yet to read.

Aged twenty one, with dreams of being a cowboy running through his head, he travelled to British Colombia and drifted around North America but returned to British Colombia where he worked in a store. He mentioned to a customer who was also the editor of a newspaper that he wrote poetry and the paper printed six of his poems about the Boer War, including his famous "March of The Dead". Eventually Service ended up in the Yukon where he wrote some of his most famous poems including "The Shooting of Dan McGrew."

He wrote more poems about the gold rush and the wildness of the country and eventually wrote enough to compile a small book which he sent to his father who had now immigrated to Toronto. His father took the manuscript to a printer whose workforce loved them. They sold 1700 advance copies just by a salesman reading the poems as they came from the proofs. The book was called "Songs of a Sourdough", and became a huge success in America and in the United Kingdom. He eventually earned over $100,000 from its sales. He stopped working in the bank and published another book of poetry "Ballads of A Cheechako" and then a novel "The Trail of 98". They were both huge successes. Now wealthy he was able to travel to Paris, The French Riviera and to Hollywood. In 1912 he published his third book of Poetry "Rhymes of a Rolling Stone." Service had found his audience, everything he wrote was a success. He was one of those rare things, a poet who actually made money!

In 1913, he moved to Paris and settled in the Latin Quarter posing as a painter and married a Parisian named Germain Bourgion daughter of a distillery owner. When World War One broke out he tried to enlist but due to his age (41) and having varicose veins, he was turned down. For a while he wrote for the Toronto Star before working as a stretcher bearer and ambulance driver with the American Red Cross, until he fell ill. He wrote his book of war poetry "Rhymes of a Red Cross Man" in 1916. It's dedicated to one of his brothers who had been killed in action.

At the end of the war Service carried on living in Paris when in daytime he would wear suits and sport a monocle whilst at nights would dress in old clothes and visit the lowest Parisian dives, the inspiration for his next book of poetry called "Ballads of Bohemia".

During World War II he moved to California and worked alongside Hollywood stars to "help the morale of the troops" by visiting Army Camps and reading his poetry. In 1942 he was even asked to play himself in a movie called "The Spoilers" starring John Wayne, Marlene Dietrich and Randolph Scott. When the war was over he returned to Brittany where he lived until 1947 when he upped sticks and moved to Monaco and wrote the two volumes of his autobiography "Ploughman of the Moon" and "The Harper of Heaven." He died in 1958 in Lancieux where he is buried in the local cemetery. I mean what a guy, what a life, what a writer, what a poet! Of course I was inspired by him. Of course I wanted to be a poet. For a while I wanted to be Robert W. Service himself.

In the late 1960's maybe even the early 70's a favourite singer of mine, one Country Joe McDonald ex-lead singer of Country Joe and The Fish, put some of Robert Services' poetry to music and issued it as an album. It's called "War, War, War" and I searched for years for a copy. Of course now you can call it up anytime you want on Spotify. Give it a listen, even better buy a copy of the poems of Robert W. Service.

So I wrote and generally carried on life as any other teenager in the so called swinging 60's did. In addition to being influenced by the many writers I was reading I was also influenced by musicians, by The Beatles (wasn't everyone?), The Pink Floyd, The Lovin' Spoonful, The Bonzo Dog Doo Dah Band, The Rolling Stones, Bob Dylan, The Kinks, The Doors, The Byrds, Jefferson Airplane, Otis Redding and the television music show "Ready Steady Go".

However writing the words just wasn't enough. It's hard to explain but looking back, I've always had this thing about my art and my writing. Just doing it isn't enough. My poetry isn't written just to leave in a note book, or typed up and left brooding, neatly filed away in some cupboard. For me I had the feeling that poetry needed to be performed, to be spoken out loud. The only problem was where? I went to enough party's where teenage wanna be Bob Dylan's would take their guitars along and sit on the staircase, playing covers or self written material, mostly badly. A situation brilliantly lampooned in the movie "Animal House." It was just like that at many 1960's parties, only no one actually smashed the guitar, although many deserved it.

The late 60's parties were no different to ones today, drinkers would congregate in the kitchen, the guys wanting to get off with the girls would be dancing in the living room, and the intense ones sat on the staircase listening to someone play Bob Dylan badly, blocking the way to the toilet and forcing anyone who wanted to go upstairs to push passed. It was bad enough if you wanted to go to the loo, but even more embarrassing for the couple who had just "got it together" and were trying to sneak off for some privacy into one of the bedrooms. This happened more than you'd think. Of course the pill was now in use and the sexual revolution was kicking in, even in the suburbs of Leeds.

I remember an unfortunate incident at a party where I met a very willing young lady and we ventured upstairs. I think we were in the parent's bedroom. As she undressed and we lay on the bed she suddenly sat bolt upright and announced that she was going to be sick. Mindful of being in the parental bedroom I quickly leapt out of bed and flung a window open. She followed, leant out and promptly and profusely vomited. Once she had finished I led her back to the bed where she lay back and fell asleep. I left her to it and returned to the kitchen just as a friend of mine came in through the back door. He had the remains of vomit on him and was not a happy person. I asked him what happened.

"I was outside with a girl, we were snogging against the back of the house and I was just got my hand up her blouse when a window opened and someone threw up all over us!"

I murmured my commiserations but couldn't stop laughing all the home. It was love and peace fuelled by John Smiths Bitter, Babycham, and the occasional quid deal of low quality hashish.

Sometimes the parties were of the "let's smoke some dope, sit in the dark, listen to Bob Dylan, talk about Vietnam, peace, love and how we could change the world" variety, where you tried to pull by sheer intellectualism.

Sometimes the parties were more mod based, where there was alcohol, soul music, dancing and a whole heap of pills to see you through the night.

Which party you went to, depended on which group you hung around with. Me? I hung around with them all. Well the mod's had the better looking, more fashion conscious girls, but the dope smoking group, who would eventually morph into the hippies, tended to attract a more heady, sexually active type of girl. Sometimes at these parties someone, usually someone older than me, would read a poem. It wasn't me. I was much too unsure of myself and my writing to take that type of risk.

Then I discovered a whole new sub-culture, the folk music scene. When I say folk music I don't mean the Bob Dylan and the Donovan's, I mean the real McCoy. I mean the Ewan MacColl's and the Alex Campbell's. I mean the hardened ale drinkers and the bearded Arran sweater wearers. The folkies had emerged from the late 50's Beatnik scene and tended to congregate in small back rooms of public houses where the singers would sing a selection of contemporary and traditional songs, sometimes with guitars sometimes with banjos and sometimes unaccompanied.

I discovered this particular phenomenon one evening in an upstairs room in a small village pub called The Black Swan in a village called Barwick-in-Elmet, a few miles bus ride up the road from where I lived. At first glance the place was intimidating. I was around seventeen and found myself in a dark, upstairs room where the tables were beer barrels, candles provided the lighting, the audience older and who all seemed to know each other, plus know all the words to all the songs that anyone who got up to sing, and they all joined in on the choruses! Even worse was that, as an audience member you were expected to contribute to the night by not talking. You were expected to treat every performer and their material with a reverend hush. People even tutted if the door was opened mid-song and light and noise spilled into the room from the downstairs public bar.

The Black Swan Folk Club had a regular folk group called Penda's Way who hosted and performed at the start and end of each night. The bit in the middle was filled by a succession of, what was then called, floor singers. These days the entire night would be called an "open-mic" night. Occasionally the club would feature a booked singer, a "professional" folk singer who got paid for around an hours' worth of performance, plus encores. Of course for these nights there was a charge. If you wanted to see the professional you had to pay. I suppose it was run a bit like a working man's club, only Arran sweaters replacing the half time pies. Strangely enough, for one so hung up on pop and rock music I found myself drawn to the folk club, it's singers and its songs. It was refreshing. I liked the songs the singers sang. I liked the lyricism. I realised I'd just discovered another form of poetry. I found that I liked the traditional songs, especially the ones about work and long gone strikes, ones about industrial unrest or the protest songs about bad working practices. I loved the mining songs, the weaving songs, the songs about the navvies and canal builders, the railway navvies, songs about poverty, songs about strikes. Then it hit me. I was hearing words not written by modern or professional songwriters, but songs with words written by ordinary working people way back in the 18th and 19th centuries. These were real words written by real people about real situations. Despite the fact they were sung by modern folkies these lyrics were the voices of past generations speaking to me over the years. Of course there were also ballads, mostly about lost love and dead lovers, or even worse, lovers that had been kidnapped by the army of navy and dragged off to some distant land to fight for King and Country. There was also a smattering of comedy songs, material that had their origins in the Edwardian music halls. I had found a new vein of poetry and poetry probably more authentic than much of the stuff I had listened to so far. Intrigued and inspired with this new found mine of culture I even bought myself a copy of A. L. Lloyd's book "Folk Song In England."

One night I took my courage, all fortified by a couple of pints of John Smith's Bitter, to Tony Aked the singer with Penda's Way and the bloke that ran the club.

"Can I get up and do a couple of poems?" I asked.

To my great surprise he said yes. That was my first ever public performance. I can still remember standing up at the front, hoping that no one would notice my shaking. Fat chance, I was reading it off the paper (I still do), and the paper was waving around like some sort of signal flag. Anyway I got through it and received a smattering of applause for my efforts. Tony said it was OK and that I was welcome to do it again the following week. I did, and did the week after. I'm not too sure what I performed in that club, but I do know that one I did perform a bit later was a poem called "Horace the Pigeon". I still figure it was the most decent thing I had written up to that point. Here it is -

Horace the Pigeon
Once upon a time, far out in t' Dales
there was this here pigeon called Horace,
now Horace being an unusual sort of pigeon
thought he'd like to see more of the world,
so he flew down Aire Valley
looking at Keighley, Shipley, and Bingley
but, as he didn't reckon much to them
passed onto Leeds and Hunslet,
and thought he were in some sort of Hell.

Now Horace flew round in a circle,
cos all grime and all soot and all muck
had clogged up most of his feathers,
and he were feeling reet out of luck.
Till at last he came into Bradford,
at least he assumed he were there
cos a dollop of summat got him reet in t'eye
and he couldn't see owt at all.
Then suddenly CRASH,
and with a bloody great Splat,
he flew into t'town hall wall
and poor Horace was sadly demised.

This story was told with sheer horror,
by pigeons from far and from wide,
and that's why if you're ever in Bradford,
and you take a peep up into skies,
all pigeons are flying arse forward,
to keep bloody muck from their eyes.
Graham Rhodes circa 1967/8

Sometimes in the late 60's just after I had discovered it, the Black Swan Folk Club moved. It left the upstairs room in the small village pub in Barwick and took residency a few miles away, in a pub called The Seacroft, which unsurprisingly, was in a suburb of Leeds called Seacroft. The pub was a modern, early 60's building and sold Davenport's beer, which was unusual as Davenports was the beer that was usually sold in home deliveries "Beer at Home means Davenports!" as the old advert used to say.

Once Seacroft had been a small village with a row of cottages, a pub, a church and a village green, then in the early sixties Leeds swallowed it up and surrounded it with council estates, a shopping centre and bus station. It was situated on the ever widening A64 to York and a section of the Leeds Ring Road. In the mid sixties I used to go to the Seacroft Youth Club deep in the concrete bowels of the shopping centre. It was rough but alright, but it opened just as I was leaving youth clubs behind in favour of sneaking into underage drinking pubs and gigs, and folk clubs.

More importantly to me the folk clubs new location was within a reasonable, walkable, distance from my home. Obviously I still lived with my parents in a thirties built house with a large garden at the Leeds end of Barwick Road where a pair of metal gates proudly proclaimed it to be "Burnside". Which it was. A small stream flowed alongside a muddy path that ran between the stream and our hedge. As a kid it was a great playground. At the other side of the stream was a small hill suitable for sledging in winter, that ran up to a railway embankment, a loop line from Leeds to Wetherby that Dr Beeching closed in 1964. Just down from our house there were two bridges. One was where the stream passed under Barwick Road and twenty yards on, another allowed the railway to cross the road. I used to practice rock climbing on the rough stone that supported the bridge and as a dare, would squat down between the two girders at the top of the bridge as a steam engine rattled past.

The stream also played an important part in my life. I used to dam it just under the bridge so the water would build up into a deep pool. I would wade in it, throw stones in it, fly over it on a rope swing, even fall into it. My Grandfather told me that once the stream was a river and that twice it ran red with blood. Years later I checked his story out and he was right. The house where we lived was right on the site of an ancient battle between King Oswy of Northumberland and King Penda of Mercia that determined the fate of Christianity in the North. Penda and his men had to cross the river and were attacked by the Northumbrians who chose that moment to sweep down on them. The Mercians were defeated and as a result, Whitby Abbey got build and York Minster was renovated. The second time the river ran red with blood was much further downstream, at Towton, the battle in the War of the Roses. Fought in a snowstorm on Palm Sunday it has the dubious record of the greatest number of deaths that ever occurred in a battle in the United Kingdom.

The new Seacroft Folk club, still hosted by the band Penda's Way, ran on a Wednesday night and was situated in a large back room of the pub, more suitable to cabaret or a cheap working man's club, which on other nights of the week, it emulated. Despite losing its rustic, village pub quaintness not only did the club survive, it flourished. The club attracted a new and larger audience and could now afford a "guest" performer almost every week. Some were the newly established Yorkshire singers, like Dave Burland, Jake Thackeray and the brilliant Tony Capstick. Some were from further afield, Lancashire, Teeside or Scotland. Believe it or not Seacroft Folk Club actually saw performances by the likes of Vin Garbutt, Mike Hardin, Eddie and Finbar Furey, Bob Williamson and Billy Connelly, before they all became famous, and in some cases, before they left folk music behind to become stand-up comedians. A period in their early careers when they were young men that sang folk songs and their wit and humour was kept to the in-between song banter. Mike Harding sang songs of industrial Manchester and about the cotton mills. Jake Thackeray was just about to burst on our television screens courtesy of Bernard Braden. Billy Connelly was singing in such a broad Scots accent that we didn't really know what he was singing about, the same with Vin Garbutt from Middlesbrough, who not surprisingly had a strong Teeside accent, and sang mainly his own material that was shortly to appear on his first album "Valley of the Tees." Well worth a listen. He also recorded at least a dozen other albums before his untimely death in 2017.

In my opinion back then, the wittiest of them all was Bob Williamson. He didn't sing many folk songs instead he had an act of comic and parody songs. A song praising "Holland's Meat Pies" was a parody of the Everly Brothers song "Ebony Eyes." "The Folky" was a parody of Paul Simons "The Boxer". In 1976 he released a single called "Kippers For Tea" a brilliant parody of Brotherhood of Man's Eurovision winner "Save Your Kisses For Me".

He even performed monologues, carrying on that great Lancashire monologue tradition. Here I must hold my hand up and admit to pinching a couple. I've no idea where Bob got them from but both "Aggie The Elephant" and "Jonathan Cooper" have been in my act ever since. When I moved to Harrogate he played the folk club there and stayed the night at my flat paying for his bed and breakfast with a crate of beer. I think that was the night he taught me the monologue "Jonathan Cooper". To this day it still makes people laugh. It's served me well for over 50 years. Bob was tipped to be big, and in the early 1970's even had a TV special broadcast. He was a regular on the Wheeltappers and Shunters Social Club television programme and appeared in a talent show episode of Coronation Street but unfortunately he had to cut back on his live work after sustaining a back injury falling down the stairs, so he turned to writing scripts for TV, radio, and fellow comics. He did have a cameo role at the end of some episodes of Peter Kay's Phoenix Nights, the auditions bit. He also set up the Swell Acts Agency. Unfortunately his career was cut short when he was diagnosed with a rare blood disorder. He died aged 67 in 2016.

Jonathan Cooper

When Jonathan Cooper
came home from school
he started to cry, and to cry
he cried and he cried
for nearly three weeks
and his mam started wondering why

"What's matter young John ?" his mother did say"
have you been caught in the bike shed again
or have you been given the stick
for playing at darts with your pen ?"

"Oh no" Young Jonathan said,
"it's nothing like that
It's all got to do with me willie
we were measuring in showers just after games

and mine were so small it looked silly"

*"Right", said his mum
"Down to gypsies we'll go
some of his spells we shall borrow
I reckon he'll make it grow long right away,
you'll be tripping over bugger tomorrow"*

*Next morning at gypsies
young John showed his complaint
it were certainly nothing to boast
and gypsy at first thought he'd sprouted a worm,
and then he prescribed John, hot toast.*

*"Hot toast", said his Mam
"Have you gone bloody mad,
it's his willie that's lacking you twit,
why, just look at poor little thing hanging there
at tea time I ate bigger chips."*

*"It's a common complaint, Mrs Cooper", he said
"and mostly men, don't you know,
but nature has found best cure of them all,
cos hot buttered toast makes them grow".*

*Next morning at breakfast, young John he came down,
he looked like he'd just seen a ghost,
cos on every plate, and piled up to t'roof,
were hundreds of pieces of toast.*

*"I can't eat all them, mam" Jonathan said
and his face grew morbid and sad.
"It's all right love, there's only two slices for you,
rest of em's all for your Dad".*

Bob Williamson

Tony Capstick was also screamingly funny. Whilst he was a prolific drinker, he always held the audience at any folk club in the palm of his hand. I remember one gig where he was told not to swear as it was being broadcast live on the local radio station. He managed right up to the end when, thinking the program had ended he finished, swore profusely and vomited. Unfortunately the radio was still broadcasting. Tony was much more than a comedian. He was an excellent singer and brilliant interpreter of folk songs both contemporary and traditional. The flip side of his hit record "Capstick Comes Home", a parody of the Ridley Scott Hovis advert, is a traditional song called "The Sheffield Grinder" check it out sometime, only find the version without the brass band. His recordings with the band Hedgehog Pie are also well worth a listen. For over thirty years he was a presenter on Radio Sheffield and for a number of years was one of the policemen in the long running TV series "The Last of The Summer Wine." He died aged 59 in 2009.

I can remember the other performers that headlined whilst I did my little five minute floor spot at the Seacroft Folk Club. There was a young man called Trevor Midgley, who performed under the name of Beau, he was one of the first people I saw that played a twelve string guitar. In 1969 he was signed by "Dandelion", John Peel's record label who released Beau's first album. On it were a number of the songs we had heard him perform at the Seacroft club throughout the previous year. One track was a firm favourite. It was called "1917 Revolution" and, as the title indicated, it was a song about the Russian revolution. In fact it was so good that "Dandelion" released it as a single. It didn't worry the charts in the UK but some copies made it to The Lebanon of all places, just as a real life revolution was underway. For some reason best known to themselves the revolutionaries liked the record and bought it, sending it to number one in the Lebanese charts. To date it's the only number one record the "Dandelion" label ever achieved. Of course it goes without saying that neither the label nor Beau ever received a penny from its success. Beau carried on singing and recording while maintaining a serious, non musical career. Now in his sixties he's still writing and singing and is releasing albums on a yearly basis. You can find them all on his web site and on Spotify.

I also befriended another folk singer, a friend of Beau's, a Jewish folk singer from Leeds that tended to cover Tom Paxton songs and had a couple of his own songs that were pretty decent. His name was Dave Abrams, and we'll hear much more of him later on in my story.

There was another act that enjoyed my poetry, a female duo from Liverpool called Jackie and Bridie. In fact they liked it so much they invited me to perform at their club. It was called The Coach and Horses and was in an area of Liverpool called Toxteth. I took up their invitation and travelled there just the once. It was an amazing night and one that made me realise I still had a very long way to go as a writer. The duo sang a wide variety of material, comedy and traditional songs. Some like "Glencoe", would bring a tear to your eye, whilst others like "Will They Ever Bridge the Humber?" had you falling off your chair with laughter. It was at that one visit to their club I saw a poet that, to this day, still inspires me despite the fact I've never read a word he wrote. He was introduced as Arthur the Poet. His real name was Arthur Williams and he was a docker, and although he was funny, it wasn't the humour that got to me. It was his way of writing, his choice of words. He used the everyday language of the working class, the ordinary words that the dockers that worked around him used. Up to that point in my life I had never come across a poet who used everyday language to express themselves. Even the

Liverpool poets sometimes used a lexicon to flower up their language. Like I said, I've never read anything he wrote. I'm not even sure if he was ever published, but his short ten-minute performance that I saw that night has affected my writing and concept of poetry for the last fifty years. One line of his that's stuck in my had was from a bit of his work called Dockers Nicknames and I sincerely wish I could remember more of it.

"There was "Wonder Boy" cos everything he unloaded he would say "I wonder what's in this?

Then there was "Spaceman", we called him that cos every night he would say I'm off to Ma's for me tea!"
Arthur the Poet, a true poet of the people.

Of course it wasn't just folk songs and folk singers that inspired my writing. The late 60's gave birth to many great contemporary singer/songwriters who's words inspired me. First and foremost there was Roy Harper who's two albums "Come Out Fighting Ghengis Smith." (released in 1968) and "Folkjokeopus." (released in1969), not only inspired my writing but also changed my entire way of thinking. I think side two of "Ghengis Smith" taught me more about life than school or work ever did.

Then there were the songs of Paul Simon with the "Bookends" album released by Simon and Garfunkel in 1968. There was Al Stewart with his albums "Bed Sitter Images" (1967) and "Love Chronicles" (1969), two albums that provided not only a blueprint to life, but also a blueprint on how to write great narrative lyrics. There was also Tom Rush, an American folk singer that sang traditional and contemporary American material as well as writing some great songs of his own.

Live music also played a huge part in my life. Friday nights were usually spent at the gigs held at Leeds Polytechnic College. It was there I saw Syd Barrett's Pink Floyd, Leon Russell, The Nice, Fairport Convention, Roy Harper, Chicken Shack, The Bonzo Dog Doo Dah Band, Mathews Southern Comfort, and many others.

Saturday nights, if you could blag a ticket, were spent at the Leeds University Students Union gig. There I saw the Moody Blues, Traffic, Joe Cocker, and stood outside for the legendary Who Live at Leeds gig as I couldn't get a ticket.

Every so often there were also gigs at Leeds Town Hall. Quintessence, Jethro Tull, Steeleye Span, John Mayall and many other tours Other Leeds music venues were the BG club in White Horse Street and the Three Coins a sort of nightclub in Upper Mill Hill. I always find it amusing to remember that I saw a band called the Four Pennies in a club called "The Three Coins"! I went to as many as I could afford soaking in the performances. Whilst friends and other members of the audience gasped at the guitar playing I sat there listening to the lyrics. I suppose my lack of knowledge of music, my not being able to tell one note from another, pushed me in that direction. A lot of unkind people also told me that was why I liked Captain Beefheart and Frank Zappa. Hey ho, each to their own.

So what was it like performing poetry all those years ago? Well interestingly enough it was fine. Poets were as accepted in folk clubs as were the rest of the floor singers, although they were few and far between. In fact, apart from a few performers narrating some monologues, I can't remember any other poets getting up to perform. The monologues they spoke were mainly the ones from Lancashire, made famous in the 1950's by Stanley Holloway and written mainly by Marriot Edgar, a professional pantomime dame. They were monologues like "Albert and The Lion.", "The Runcorn Ferry." "The Battle of Hastings." and "The Magna Charter." – brilliant all of them.

In fact when I think about it a lot of performers recited monologues but few ever performed poems. So what's the difference between the two? Well that question opens up a whole can of worms. To this day I'm not sure. I once asked the question in a forum on the internet, and the ensuing argument carried on alarmingly. To this day I'm still not sure. To my way of thinking everything I've ever written or at least ever performed could easily be classified as a monologue. Perhaps there really isn't a difference. I think I'll leave it to others to decide.

Chapter Two – Harrogate
1970-1977

Time moved on. I was ready to move out of the parental home. Ruth, my long term girlfriend and I wanted to live together, but parental opposition from both sides, meant we had to get married. A church wedding was arranged for Seacroft church in the summer of 1971, but we actually left Leeds and went to live in Harrogate in 1970. I had found a large attic flat on Victoria Road that overlooked Harrogate's famous Stray. I managed to get a transfer from W.H. Smith, from Leeds Bookstall to the Harrogate shop and was working in the book department. It was a lot less exciting than the bookstall. There it was a three week shift system. One week would be earlies, 5.00am to 12.00pm, then the day shift 9.00am to 5.00pm and finally the night shift 3.;0pm to 9.00pm. Starting the early shift you would have to persuade the rough sleepers to move from the piles of unpacked papers. You see they were still warm from the Yorkshire Post presses that were just up the road. You had to unpack the papers, bet them ready for the newspaper boys, whose name was a laugh as everyone of them was over 60. Indeed one actually collapse on the round. If any of them didn't turn up you would have to shoulder the sack of papers and delver the papers to various offices around Leeds City Centre, which wasn't bad. It was interesting watching the city wake up. I used to watch the sunrise from the top of City House the tower block over the City Station. Sometimes it wasn't fun like the time I got stuck in a lift in an old Victorian building. It was one of those metal cage type of lifts so as people arrived they were treated to watch me go up and down through the five floors, all of them shouting ineffectual advice. Eventually a maintenance man turned up and switched the power off leaving me to crawl out between two floors.

Saturdays in the bookstall was also a nightmare, especially when Leeds United were playing at home and the rival teams supporters arrived by train. One Saturday we were attacked by Manchester United fans welding hammers. Along with the rest of the staff I hid in the manager's office as the mob wrecked the bookstall. When we emerged the windows were smashed and half the stock along with three of the tills had disappeared.

So, whilst I spent my days in the calm and quiet of the Harrogate book department, Ruth became a receptionist in the Co-op hairdressers. Leeds friends would travel across to spend weekends with us when the flat became a sort of open house. By now, in addition to writing, I was becoming an artist of sorts. I couldn't paint to save my life, although I tried, but I could draw. I was good at pen and ink drawings and was managing to get my work into a couple of small galleries in Leeds and Harrogate. They sold and I was seriously considering giving up my job at W.H. Smiths to do it full time.

One weekend a Leeds acquaintance called Dave arrived with another called Dilly (aka Andy Robson). Dave Pruckner and Andy Robson were to play a large part in my life for the next five years, Dave more than Dilly. Both of them wrote poetry and together they had produced a small hand-made booklet of their work. They had called it Krax and they had distributed it around a few Leeds book shops. I seem to remember they sold me a copy. I read it. The content was excellent but I felt that the printing and cover needed a touch of professionalism. That night the three of us decided to produce a second copy. Dave and Andy chose the content, and graciously included a couple of mine to put in it, I typed out the content and designed and drew the cover. We scraped some money together and took the lot down to the Harrogate branch of Quickprint. A week later edition number two was ready. In order to save money we had opted to staple the thing together ourselves, a cost saving but time consuming exercise. Andy took some through to Leeds whilst Dave and I hawked the rest around Harrogate. We managed to distribute them and made plans for a third edition.

Some poems from the second edition of Krax –

Drunk on Poetry
You can get drunk on poetry
Dilly Robson said
If you read it fast enough
It goes straight to your head
So I'll have glass of Milton
And maybe a bottle of Shelley
And then we'll take a crate of Wordsworth
Back to my place and watch telly.
Do you fancy Bacardi and Coleridge
Maybe Adrian Henri on ice
Have a quick sip of Roger McGough
Brian Pattern with a cherry would be nice!

You can get drunk on poetry
At least that's what I've heard
So get hold of a volume of Byron
And drink up every word.
But here's a word of warning
-It could lead to much harder stuff
And, if you're not careful
On Homer and Virgil you'll get hooked

So turn on a friend to poetry
You'll find it most inviting
But please to heed a final word
Don't drink when you've been reciting!
You know it makes sense!
Dave Pruckner

The Barrenness of Da Cunha
So tell me I'm not an island,
Not an unclimbed rock of emotion
Why not?

My dreams protect what I desire
My hopes forever dashed in the mighty waves
Of truth and reality, movement and change.
I take my loves within me
(Only then can I be sure I exist of myself)
I have more grief within my soul
That can ever be pent up
And never released.

Tomorrow there will be earthquakes;
For only the whims of time and fate
Can cause the eruption that is aching to begin
Andy Robson

Looking back at the second edition back I think there's some decent stuff in there, although I have to admit, I'm a bit embarrassed at some of the illustrations, but that was then!

By 1972 Dave had moved into the Harrogate flat and taken up residency in the spare room. Having sold all the copies of Krax 2 we got ambitious. Despite having a steady flow of material coming in from readers we decided to write to Roger McGough. I've no idea how we found an address but we sent off a letter and a copy of the second edition. Some weeks later we got an answer. Yes he would contribute and to prove it he included some in the letter. It was two of his unpublished vampire poems.

When I fly
I keep close to chimneystacks
And gutted warehouses
Hovering just out of reach
Of men's anger.
I take off from bombsites
And model my technique
On litter
Caught in the wind

During the day
I camouflage myself
To blend against a thousand backgrounds
All grey.

My fear
Is that one morning
When I have landed
To refuel with sorrow
They will capture me
Tie my wings behind my back
And drive a stake through my fuselage.
Roger McGough

In the same issue we also published a poem by Brian Pattern. It was called Angel Wings and I've no idea how we got our hands on it. Probably we wrote to him as well. Krax, our little magazine, had achieved a publishing scoop. I think we doubled our print run for that issue. However, no matter how successful the magazine was, for me publishing wasn't enough. I missed performing. Dave and I had come back from the pub and were listening to some music, we were probably drunk. "Let's form a poetry band!" I remember saying. He nodded. We had no idea of what we were letting ourselves in for, or what adventures lay ahead.

We put the word out and fixed a rehearsal venue and time. It was to be a Sunday afternoon, at the West Yorkshire Road Car Social Club, just down from the Harrogate's Odeon cinema. As far as I can remember the first participants were Pin (aka Mick Richardson) and Bernie McTeigue, two guitar playing friends from Leeds. Then there was a guy who worked as a picture framer called Colin Vale, who played guitar and mandolin, another guy called Steve Morrison a singer and guitarist, and Dave and myself. We named the band after the magazine and rehearsed a couple of times before we were joined by another guitarist and a drummer. I think we must have put an advert in the local newspaper as one day we answered the flat door to find two guys stood there asking if we were the people looking for musicians. We were. They introduced themselves as Pete Cosker, guitarist and his mate Dave Peacock, a drummer. We explained we weren't looking for a drummer but the guitarist said they came together so we gained a drummer. In these early days they didn't have anywhere to live and so they both crashed in my flat for a while. I think it was Pete tha5t got the carpet in front of the fireplace.

Now the band was beginning to take shape and, although Bernie dropped out, it sort of gelled. We actually did a couple of gigs before being joined by a young girl who had either just left school or was still attending. Her name was Julianne Mumford. We had met her when she had called around to the flat with some of her poems and an illustration for the magazine. They were good and we had printed them.

Don't stay if you don't want to
Have some coffee
Make yourself at home
Yes, it's rather late.
But there's a good programme on T.V.
Oh, I see.
Well some other time then
Yes. Well. Goodbye then. Ciao.

And the emptiness of the house
Makes the walls as thin as matchboxes
And the glass like cellophane
Vibrating with the noise of the car leaving.

I wish he'd stayed. But he didn't
And the void in the house is like
The one in your eyes.
Slowly filling only with the black syrup of
Sleep.
Alone.
Julie Mumford

As far as I can remember she stayed with the band for a few months, maybe it was longer. She disappeared with some bikers and ended up moving to Bradford where she carried on writing and drawing. Not so many years later she re-emerged as Joolz the Punk poetess, living with and illustrating the covers for the band The New Model Army. She even got a publishing deal and a recording contract, I used to have a single by her tucked away somewhere. Now called Joolz Denby, over the years she has been really successful with appearances at Glastonbury and other major events. She even has her own Wikipedia page! I mean that's status for you. It's just a pity that it doesn't acknowledge her beginnings with Krax magazine who first published her work and Krax the band with whom she did her first appearances. Here's a resume of her from a festival program –

Joolz Denby is a writer, poet, spoken-word performer, illustrative and fine artist, curator, photographer and tattooist, ...and she's going to be at this year's festival.

Her poetry collections include The Pride of Lions (1994), Errors of the Spirit (2000), and Pray For Us Sinners, a book of short stories and poems published in 2005. Her first novel, Stone Baby, won the **1998 Crime Writers' Association New Crime Writer of the Year** *and was shortlisted for the Crime Writers' Association John Creasey Memorial Dagger. Her novel, Billie Morgan (2004), was shortlisted for the Crime Writers' Association Dagger in the Library Award and the Orange Prize for Fiction. Her most recent novels are Borrowed Light (2006), set in a Cornish surfing village, A True Account Of The Curious Mystery Of Miss Lydia Larkin & The Widow Marvell (2011) and Wild Thing (2012), about an urban feral child.*

Joolz also works in the music industry, as a recording artist, illustrative artist for **New Model Army***, and manager of the young Bradford band, New York Alcoholic Anxiety Attack. Her touring exhibition, One Family, One Tribe – The Art and Artefacts of New Model Army, is a collection of her 25 years of artwork for the legendary cult rock band. Her photographic exhibition/installation, Bradford – True North, was shown at Bradford University in 2006, and she is curating an exhibition on elective body modification – The Body Carnival – for Bradford's Cartwright Hall Gallery. Joolz was Artistic Director of Illuminate's Radical Brontë Festival in 2006 and was designated a Cultural Revolutionary in the North of England for her* *contribution to the region's Arts. Joolz is well-known for her work in prisons and with marginalized young people and has performed her work all over the world, and broadcasts on* **BBC Radio 1 and Radio 4.** *She lives in Bradford.*

For a performance poet who started with Krax she has done remarkably well. When I was living in York, in the late nineties I went to one of her gigs at Waterstone's bookshop. Her poetry was powerful, it always had been.

Our first (and only) gig as a nine piece band was at Skipton Town Hall. Julianne Mumford was gigging with us and as a result of her connections with the leader of a biker gang, the first two rows of the audience were full of leather clad bikers, the majority of which were obviously wishing they were somewhere else. However they were soon treated to a spectacle that distracted them from the so called literature and provided them with an unexpected entertainment. We never realised the Dave Peacock, the drummer had a drink problem until halfway through the gig when he suddenly, and unexpectedly collapsed over his drum kit. We managed to drag him off stage and deposit him in a dressing room hoping he would sleep it off. We returned to the stage for a second half and seemed to be going down alright when we became aware that the audience were not looking at us. They were looking up above our heads. We looked up and realised, with a certain amount of horror that our drummer had woken up and found his way back to the stage. Not only that but somehow he had managed to climb up the curtains and was now swinging hand over hand on the lighting rig hanging above the stage. Some of the band attempted to carry on playing and us poets continued spouting our words whilst others tried to persuade him to climb down. It was obvious that the audience were oblivious to what the performers were attempting to do. The real show was watching the non playing members of the band in their failed attempts to persuade the drummer to come down off the lighting rig. Eventually his arms must have tired because he got down. The rest of the band grabbed him and dragged him backstage once again. I'm not sure if we actually did it but I'm certain I heard someone suggest tying him up till it was time for us to leave.

Another stand out gig was at some college miles away from Harrogate. For the occasion we borrowed a van and a guy called Brian that was acting as a roadie for us and other bands. Sure enough the old transit van broke down halfway to the venue. Fair play to the roadie, he climbed out and lifted the bonnet. The rest of us got out and mooched around, passing a joint around between us, trying not to look anxiously at out watches. After around fifteen minutes he announced it was trouble with the electrics and he had narrowed it down to the spark plugs. He stripped them out and then asked for a cigarette packet. One was produced and he ripped it apart and took out the silver foil that he then proceeded to place into the spark plugs. He fixed it all up and slammed down the bonnet. The van started up first time and we made it to the venue around an hour late, but still in time to do the gig. We found a backstage jobsworth who rushed around and directed us to a stage curtained off from the audience that we could hear at the other side applauding another act on the bill. We hardly had time to get the gear onstage, plug it in and switch it on before we could hear the MC's voice loudly proclaim,

"Tonight's band, please welcome Krax".

The curtains swished back and there we were on stage looking at the backs of around a hundred or so students. Dave Pruckner was the first to react. He tapped the mic in front of him and quietly said,

"Excuse me, we're behind you!"

There was a strange sort of pause as the realisation struck and the audience all shuffled around to face us. It turned out there were two stages in that hall, and the over eager jobsworth had put us on the wrong one.

Drink played a very large part in our lives back then, as did dope but that wasn't unusual among the musicians, artists and the vast majority of the all the other young people in town. However many of the more "adult" oriented pubs in Harrogate were wary of the long haired hippies and we weren't welcome in a lot of them. At one point I think we were restricted to the bar at the Alex (The Alexandria) and the back room bar at The Crown Hotel. Hence a young artist cum musician called Graham Cardy found a back room at a down at heel Harrogate pub called the Cock and Castle where he founded a weekly series of what can only be described as "happenings", where musicians would jam and play, poets would rant whilst in the background artists would paint large backdrops. Today it would probably be classified as an open mic, only back then it was looser and more disorganised. Looking back I can remember that back room as a dark, noisy, smoke-filled, grubby place where Johnny Middleton (Harrogate's finest artist) was forever painting a backdrop, where ashtrays were always full, the atmosphere reached industrial standards of smoke pollution and the floor was always swimming with split beer. It was a spit and sawdust place where the sawdust was the previous night's furniture. Perhaps I'm doing the place an injustice, perhaps I'm not. Personally I've always preferred watching bands in pubs with a cigarette in one hand, a pint in the other and where my feet stuck to the floor. I know that Dave and I read our poetry there on more than one occasion, but I'm not sure that the band ever played there. It was in that back room of the Cock and Castle that another band began to form and play. They called themselves Wally which started off as a fluid group of musicians centred around a singer songwriter called Roy Webber. In fact I remember that at the start they didn't have a drummer, they had Johnny Middleton hitting a variety of tin trays as his brother Paul played an old beaten up pedal steel guitar doubling up sometimes on guitar or bass. The nights at the Cock and Castle were rowdy, explosive and full of musical talent and enthusiasm. Sometime in the 90's the place was pulled down and the site is now covered by the loading bay for Marks & Spencer's. I wonder if the ghosts of the past still wander around looking for a decent pint and some good times. Probably not!

To this day I'm not sure if that first Krax band was actually any good. For a start I'm not too sure about my own material. This is a poem of mine from the Cock and Castle and Krax mark one period. I remember it was written by candle light during a power cut at the time of the thee day week. Unfortunately it's just as relevant now as it was back then. Nothing seems to have changed.

Unemployment
I won't be going down t'mill
tomorrow on the bus
I won't be going anywhere
I'll stay at home and rest
cos I've been made redundant
they don't want no skill no more
just sixteen year old lasses
pushing buttons on t'factory floor

Still lassies gotta earn a crust
cos times are hard these days
they said they might retrain us
but I'll never change my ways

I've fettled looms for forty years
since I was just a lad

and although they paid me off quite well
I've never felt so bad

I've nowt to do - I'm fifty two
I'll never work again
no factory will employ you
when they think your over t'hill

So here I sit by t'fireside
and spit into the flames
I've done me time
but never earned enough to see me gains
I'm cast aside, rejected like
washed up at fifty two
yon mill has sucked me life away
and leaves me, sitting empty like
with bugger all to do.
Graham Rhodes circa 1972/3ish

I also remember a great poem of Dave's that always got a laugh from the audience. It was called –

Poem for the Bay City Rollers
Those blokes that manage you
Don't do things by halves
You've done bugger all for music
But you've sold a lot of tartan scarves.
Dave Pruckner

See, I told you his stuff was funny! What I can't remember are the songs and tunes that the musicians played and whether they were covers or if there was any original material among it. Perhaps that's a good thing. Anyway this first version of the Krax band soon dissolved. Pete Cosker, left to join Wally, which in hindsight was a bloody good decision. Dave the drummer left to smuggle cymbals out of Turkey, or so I seem to remember. Perhaps he didn't, perhaps that was just the alcohol talking. Colin Vale, Pin and Steve Morrison also left at the same time.

So now we were down to just the four poets.

Then, as Andy Robson recalls, we were approached by two brothers, Russell and John (surname unknown). They both played guitar and asked if they could join us. They were fine musicians but we only did one gig with them as they didn't really gel with the rest of us.

Andy also remembers the eventful rehearsal for that gig, when Julianne brought her boyfriend, John, along. He was an inventor of sorts and brought along a strange contraption of his own making. After much speculation among the rest of us, Joolz revealed that it was a bubble machine. It was filled with a solution and when a handle was turned it blew bubbles across the room. It would have been a great addition to our act had it not been for one minor flaw – John couldn't get it to work!

Now here's a strange coincidence. On Wednesday 1st September 2021, alongside two friends from a band called Northern Riots, I did a gig at Scarborough's excellent Mojo's cafe that hold acoustic gigs on Wednesday and Saturday afternoons (4 till 5). Seated at the front was a man and his wife and two children. After the gig he announced that he had seen me way back in Harrogate in the early seventies which was why he came to the gig to see if it really was me. We all went for a drink together and reminisced. He bought a copy of the first version of this book and we said goodbye. A week later I got an e-mail. It turns out that the guy was John, the John that made the bubble machine, The John that I had written about in the previous paragraph!

Back to the seventies. This gig also saw the departure of Andy Robson from the band, although he continued to be the driving force behind the Krax magazine until it ceased publication in 2014. I believe it was the longest running of any small poetry magazines. It was also around this time that Julianne also left the band.

Anyway Krax (The band) was now just Dave and myself. We did a few double headed gigs together at various Harrogate venues when we were joined by a third poet who's claim to fame was that he was the son of the famous children's writer Rosemary Sutcliffe. His name was Chris Hardwick and he lived in York.

As Dave recalls, we were doing a gig in York and going down well, when someone began to heckle us from the back of the hall. We exchanged ripostes with him for a while until he fell silent. After the gig, a guy approached us and began to apologise profusely. When he saw us looking puzzled he explained that he had been the heckler. He was a little the worse for wear, but told us he had really enjoyed the show and that he wrote poetry as well. Before we knew it we had invited him over to the flat and he'd joined us in Krax!

By now Dave and I were getting some sort of recognition. Someone in the Harrogate arts circle realised there were real living poets in Harrogate and we got a couple of try out gigs at the Harrogate Youth Theatre. It seemed that the director, an enthusiastic young man by the name of Chris Bostock liked us, liked what we did, or at least what we were trying to do, and supported our efforts to bring spoken word to the heady mix that he was offering to the theatre going public of Harrogate. We did a few poetry readings in the theatre bar as a part of his Saturday lunchtime entertainment aimed at the family shoppers. At the same time there was another young three piece band doing some music and poetry. They were a trio called Pulse. They comprised a poet called Steve Fallows, a female singer called Dee Sidwell and a guitarist and songwriter named Gar Sutton. We popped in to watch them a couple of times and they weren't bad at all.

Our third poet didn't stay with us very long, it was certainly less than a year. He ran away to join a street circus in Amsterdam, as you do and we never heard from him again. Here's a poem of his that we printed in the magazine.

THIS IS A POEM WHICH IS CALLED A POEM ENTITLED: A PLACE FOR DOING THINGS, OR DIANNE WHY DID THEY FIGHT?
Just after you wake up in the morning
And a sudden thought hits you
like a blinding blast of early sun
and you are thrown into utter misery
and the day seems very black
because suddenly you don't know
exactly what it is that causes you
to go on living.
Then at that precise moment,
as you are reaching for the bottle
of yeast tablets,
your memory serves you breakfast
and you remember that;
Spital Road, Bebington, Wirral, Cheshire,
England, Europe, The World, The Galaxy,
The Universe, Space
or wherever you happen to live
is the very place

and this is the very ripe moment
for doing the very thing
that is the ultimate reason
for your living, breathing being
that stumbles itself forward
through cornflakes and coffee
and you prepare,
with a swelling amount of love
some steaming tea
which you carry on a tray
into her room
where she lies still half asleep
and not as pretty as you remember
but gently you ask her
(and you must have waited
a long time for this)
Dianne, why did they fight?
Chris Hardwick

Dave and I carried on reading our poetry wherever we could, picking up gigs here and there, never getting paid much but expenses and free drinks were better than nothing. The magazine was still going strong and now we were both writing better material. We were also getting better known. Not by the general public but by Harrogate's various artists, musicians and other fringe performers and people outside the norm. We were booked one evening to do a gig in an upstairs room above a public library in a small market town just north of Harrogate. It was pleasant summers evening and the pair of us took to the stage in front of a small audience. What I mean is small in numbers, not in stature! It seemed to be going well enough. People laughed in the right place, applauded politely after every poem when halfway through reading a poem I received a huge thump on the side of my head that almost knocked me off my feet. I looked down at the stage to see a large cabbage rolling around. Without a pause Dave came up with one of the best ad-libs I've ever heard -

"Crackerjack!" he shouted.

The audience, who were all old enough to remember the kids TV program, burst into fits of laughter. The situation was saved. However the incident created a conundrum that I've puzzled about for the last 40 or so years. Who the hell takes a cabbage to a gig?

In more recent years I did a few gigs with a rather excellent young singer songwriter by the name of Frankie Dixon. On the first gig I told her and her mother this story about the cabbage. At our next joint gig I walked out onto the stage to find a cabbage with a painted smiley face sat on the speaker facing me.

The cabbage incident must have occurred around the same time we did a gig at a short lived Harrogate venue where, due to some bizarre licensing rules and regulations, you had to have something to eat if you wanted to drink after 10.30pm. The favourite thing among the punters was a very small, very cheap, and very nasty pizza served up on a paper plate. Everyone ordered it, but no one actually ate it. It was simply the ticket to more alcohol. Needless to say one night as I was performing someone threw their pizza at me. As it bounced off my tee-shirt I noticed there was writing on the plate. Someone had written a poem on it! The poem was eventually printed four years later, in Krax number 10, issued in 1977 long after my departure. It was titled –

"Poem on a Pizza Plate thrown at Graham Rhodes 1973".
Mist, like rainbows
Always in the distance
Drifting up the hillside

Like a priest
Rising from his knees
John Hindle

We also did a gig at the newly established Knaresborough Festival that was set up as a sort of alternative to the worlds famous Harrogate International Festival. We were booked to contribute to a night of modern poetry in the Mitre Hotel right next to Knaresborough railway station. We were joined at this gig by Andy Robson alongside some other poets that had been published by Krax magazine. Andy was on before Dave and myself, then I did my bit and Dave was last. Andy surprised both of us by walking onto the stage and producing a large witches hat that had a flashing red light beaming out of a hole cut into it. He then proceeded to read his poetry whilst repeatedly jumping backwards and forwards over the hat. Dave and I weren't the only ones to be confused. He confused the entire audience.

A couple of other poets did their thing and then it was my turn. I went up did what I did, got my applause and left the stage. There was nothing unusual or spectacular. There were few more poets and then Dave. Now I must admit some of what followed could have been my fault. Earlier in the evening I had ventured into the bar and discovered that they sold Theakstons Old Peculier, one of my favourite beers then and now. It's strong and I hadn't figured the effect it was having on Dave. By the time he got onstage he was just slightly drunk, but he managed to hold his act together and all things considered went down well. After he had finished a woman poet went up onstage. What she actually said in her introduction was

"My poetry isn't funny like the poet who was just on stage."

She then went onto explain that her poems were dedicated to

the memory of her daughter who had recently died from cancer. She then embarked on reading a series of heart wrenching painful poems that almost had the audience sobbing into their handkerchiefs.

Unfortunately in his drunken state, what Dave thought she had said was *"My poetry is funny, but not as funny as the poet who was just on stage."*

Therefore, in his drunken state he thought it would encourage her, and be beneficial to her act if he laughed very loudly after every poem. After her third poem I had to drag him outside for fear of him getting lynched. I sat him down on the pavement outside the pub and tried to explain just what a bad idea laughing at her poetry was. It took some time for the enormity of the penny to drop. Discretion being the better part of valour we decided not to go back into the gig and waited on the station for the next train back to Harrogate.

I've no idea how it happened or when but suddenly Dave and I found ourselves doing the occasional gig with the band Wally, filling in during their beer break. I think it started at the Cock and Castle and then just spread out to other gigs they did around the region. They'd do a first half, take a break, Dave and I would do around ten or fifteen minutes of poetry together and then Wally would come back onto the stage and finish their set. Back then their line-up was Roy Webber vocals and guitar, Paul Middleton pedal steel and guitar and vocals, Pete Cosker lead guitar, Alan Craig on bass, Mike Smith on drums and Paul Garret on keyboards. Some time along the way they were joined by a violinist called Pete Sage. They began playing in the Harrogate pubs and then progressed to the pub rock circuit that covered Leeds, Bradford and across the Pennines to Manchester. Soon Alan began to tire of the workload and left the band and so Paul Middleton took over on bass. In no time at all Wally was *THE* Harrogate band, its members becoming the centre of Harrogate's alternative culture. For a while its base was the back bar of the Crown Hotel at the bottom of the street called Montpellier. Just about every night of the week various members of the band would be found drinking there alongside their staunch fans. The happenings at the Cock and Castle were still going strong and Dave and I seemed to divide our time gigging there, gigging with Wally and occasionally gigging at the Harrogate Theatre. We had a PA which we shared with Wally at the start of their career and they shared their roadie Brian, who was an electrician of sorts. He would build effects pedals inside tobacco tins. They had knobs on them and a jack lead in and a jack lead out. He kept appearing with them and plugging them into the bands amps. None of them really worked and he was eventually told very severely not to bother again, when he plugged in something he'd constructed inside an old Oxo tin. Halfway through the gig it blew up and the tin spun across the stage nearly taking the singers head off.

There were other disasters. There was the Fforde Grene in Leeds. Now long demolished the Fforde Grene was in Harehills on Roundhay Road and was one of Leeds' toughest, most infamous music pubs. It hosted many bands before they became famous. In its time its hosted The Sex Pistols, U2, Simple Minds, Dire Straits and Def Leppard It's said that the Leeds band Chumbawumba wrote the song "Tubthumping" about the Fforde Grene resident drinkers. Wally played it and I went along as a roadie with another guy called Chris Hendrick a regular Wally roadie. The gig went fine, no problem. The problems arrived after the gig, just as we began to clear the stage.

"Hurry up!" Someone shouted.

"If you can do it any quicker...." Chris remarked.

Within seconds the entire occupants of the pub, tap room included, stood up and began to grab hold of the equipment and throw it through the pub windows, which were closed at the time. They didn't seem to mind if it was a guitar in its case or an amp. Everything they could lay their hands on got thrown out of the windows. I was outside in the car park, along with the band, trying to catch the equipment as it flew out of the windows in an attempt to prevent it from crashing to the floor.

Bloody Chris! He was also responsible for overloading a lift in a Bradford venue that had once been an old woollen mill. Of course the lift got stuck and we had to force open the grill and slide the equipment out through the gap between floors bit by bit until its automatic safety system freed itself and it became operational again.

At another gig, probably in Bradford, he put his hand up in order to adjust a light. He managed to shove it in a large, overhead fan that passed for air conditioning. I can still hear the sickening crunch to this day as his fingers got mangled in the spinning blades. Nothing was broken but it was severely bruised. I think we went off to the local hospital to get it sorted out for him. (At least I hope we did!).

Dave and I even travelled down to London when Wally did their first ever gig in the capital. It was at the famous Greyhound pub on Fulham Palace Road. Of course a London gig is always something special to bands working in the north. Always has been, always will be. Back then, and probably even now, northern bands and performers have this misplaced idea that every London gig is filled wall-to-wall with agents, A & R men, record company executives and other influential people in the music business. They aren't. They are full of exactly the same type of audience that the bands play to in their home town, only more discerning. I can't remember how we travelled to London but it was probably in the Wally van, a medium sized furniture van bought second hand from Boyes department store, it even had the Boyes logo still painted on the side.

We arrived at the venue late afternoon and unloaded the gear, the band set up, sound checked and we schlepped around till gig time. Wally did their first half set and just before they finished and it was time for Dave and myself, I did my usual trick of nipping off to the loo for the pre-performance piss. As I was standing there in full flow I heard a noise behind me. I turned my head and slammed it into the corner of a concrete covered water cistern. The corner got me right above my right eye. The blow almost knocked me off my feet. God it hurt, I could feel the bump swelling and the blood beginning to flow. As I leant over a grubby hand basin trying to staunch the blood and get the swelling down I heard a voice in the main room. It was announcing two poets from Harrogate. Before I left the toilet I looked around to see what had caused the noise. Inside one of the cubicles I found a person sat on a toilet, he was slumped forward. In his hand was a syringe, a band was tied tightly around his arm. His face was a shade of bluish grey. I shouted and shook his shoulder, trying to wake him up. There was no response. I didn't know what to do, I'm no medical expert but to me he looked dead. I left him where he was and left the toilet and made my way through the audience to the stage. Some helpful person had removed the stairs leading up to it. I looked up. Dave was standing at the microphone about four feet above my head, poetry in hand. I looked around and asked the members of the audience to give me a lift up. They linked their hands into a sort of stirrup, I stepped into it and they launched me upwards onto the stage. To Dave it must have looked like I had turned into some sort of jack-in-a-box. On the way up I knocked his poetry out of his hand and sent it fluttering down into the audience, who now after propelling me on the stage were now being asked to gather a number of lose sheets of paper up. It wasn't the most auspicious start to a gig, especially as I was dripping blood. As the audience grabbed at Dave's poetry and handed it back to him I tapped the microphone and spoke the following words.

"If anyone's listening at the bar, there's a body in the gent's toilet. I think someone has OD'd."

Then I added. *"This isn't part of the act and I'm not joking!"*

There was a sort of fluttering among the audience and a few people disappeared in the direction of the gents. By now the audience at the front had gathered up Dave's poetry and given it back to him so we began our performance. Dave carried on regardless. I did mine with one eye fixed onto the door of the gents, the other slowly closing. As we finished our set and were getting some applause, I saw some ambulance people enter. They came out with a stretcher. No one in the audience watched or even noticed. Wally did their second half set and went down a bomb. At the end of the gig no agents contacted us, no record company men holding out cheque books made a bee line for the band. Even more surprisingly no one from the establishment came up to speak about the toilet and it's unfortunate occupant. In fact it seemed just like it had never happened.

Recently when I was researching this book I asked Dave if it really did happen or if it was some sort of mutated memory of mine. He confirmed that I mentioned it at the time but can't remember seeing anything himself. All he remembers being too busy trying to retrieve his poetry. So did I see it or did I dream it or imagine it under some drug induced post-gig, late night reminiscence? I've no idea, but I've included it here just in case it did happen.

One of my most embarrassing moments supporting Wally was at Leeds Mechanics Institute. I'd arranged to travel through to Leeds during the day to pay a visit to my parents. Which I did. Leaving them I caught the bus into Leeds City Centre. Now remember when reading this it was the early 1970's, glam rock was on the rise. Fashion was shall we say, flamboyant. It was the age of loon pants, ridiculous flares and stack heeled, platform shoes. I was particularly proud of the pair I was wearing, they were a bit like Chelsea boots only made out of green and beige leather and had heels around three inches high. They wouldn't have looked out of place on the feet of a member of Slade. I thought they were the coolest things I'd ever worn. That was until I jumped off the moving bus at the bottom of the Headrow. I hit the road and staggered as both heels neatly snapped off both my boots. I picked them up, one was still attached by a thread of leather, it wobbled badly. The other had come right off and was laying in the gutter. I picked it up and examined it. There was no way it could be fixed back on. That night when it was time for Dave and myself to do our act I didn't walk onto the stage, I waddled on, like some weird semi-deranged penguin. You see without the heels the stack soles pointed my feet upwards. How Dave managed to do his set without laughing I've no idea. I performed mine through gritted teeth.

As Wally were gigging on a more frequent basis Roy decided that they needed a proper roadie, one who could not only drive but could act like the bands heavy. He got in touch with an old friend that he'd worked with in London, but who was actually from Consett, County Durham. His name was Stuart Pearson and on his first appearance in the Crown Bar asked Roy to point out the hardest man there. Roy pointed. Stuart walked up to him, spilt his pint and instigated an argument. Threats were made, punches thrown. Stuart returned to his seat.

"There won't be any trouble from anyone now!" he said. There wasn't.

I made friends with him at the next gig. It was at Bradford Art College fresher's ball. I don't think Dave and I read poetry at that gig. In fact I'm not sure Dave was even there. Organisation wise the whole night had been a bit of a disaster and the acts were running well late. Wally were next to last. Top of the bill was the Legs Larry Smith Band, the ex-drummer of the now defunct Bonzo Dog Band, who was discovering he wasn't as good as he thought he was. Anyway myself and Chris Hendricks were busy putting the final touches to the Wally gear. We were adjusting mics and taping down leads when there was a bit of a skirmish at the front of the stage. Someone in the now tetchy audience had heckled Paul Middleton who was minding his own business seated behind his pedal steel. God knows what was said but Paul lashed out with his foot and kicked the heckler in the head. Now if he had been wearing basket ball boots perhaps it wouldn't have been so bad, but he wasn't. He was wearing clogs, and not the high fashion Dr Scholl type of clog. He was wearing the real McCoy. Leather uppers with thick, wooden soles. The bloke on the receiving end wasn't happy with this state of affairs and went to get his mates, who, as they began to walk towards the stage, appeared to be half the audience. I noticed that Stuart had seen the incident and sussed out the situation. He climbed down from the stage and stood in the crowd, between the stage and the gathering mob. I watched and called across to Chris, who despite seeing what was happening, immediately found some vital adjustments to a mic stand that needed to be done. I turned round and tucked a couple of mic stand legs into my belt. Then I lowered myself off the stage and excusing myself to the members if the audience, made my way to where Stuart was standing. As I got behind him I tapped him on the shoulder.

"It's ok you can start, I've got your back covered!" I said and pulled out the mic stand legs.

That was all he needed he punched anything and everything in front of him. I hit a few people on the head with the mic stand legs. I couldn't have lasted more than a minute, but it was a minute that told the blokes in front of Stuart that they didn't want to be involved anymore. As they backed away he stopped and challenged them all to come outside and take him on. No one took him up on the offer. As we turned our backs and made it back to the stage he nodded his thanks. The gig was played and there was no more trouble. As we packed the gear he came across holding out his hand.

"Here's my hand, here's my heart!" he simply said.

We shook hands. We were now friends. This friendship was cemented a couple of weeks later when he separated from his wife and turned up on my doorstep with a suitcase asking if he could stay for the night. He did. In fact he stayed there for next four years. I left before he did!

Dave and I didn't gig with Wally for much longer. Despite me being a small part of their road crew I wasn't destined to be a roadie and they were aiming for much bigger and better things. It was the 1974 Melody Maker Competition that pushed them up the next rungs of rock and rolls shaky ladder of success. I think the rules said the bands had to perform three original songs. Roy picked two of his own and, much to my surprise picked one that I'd written the lyrics for. It was called "Black Crow". I don't have a copy of the words and I've no idea how the tune went, but it was inspired by my watching a crow take off from a dry stone wall and glide over a dales valley. Roy saw it as a metaphor for the American bombers flying missions across Vietnam. Anyway it was part of their set. I think the first heat, the Northern Heat, was held somewhere in Bradford, or maybe in Leeds. Where ever it was Wally sailed through along with an early roots reggae band called Jab Jab who were brilliant. They were a mixed race band who wore grass skirts and chanted and danced through the audience on their way to the stage. We all loved them. I can't remember if there were anymore heats, but the next thing I remember is a flurry of activity, much planning and arranging, and come the day a fleet of hired mini buses and cars leaving Harrogate to support Wally in the finals, held in London, at Camden's famous Roundhouse.

To everyone's disappointment Wally came second. Jab-Jab came nowhere. I have a feeling that the more sophisticated London based judges thought these Northern bands were too unsophisticated for their London susceptibilities. The winners were a band called Druid, which to this day I remember as being a bit boring. They released two albums and had an appearance on "The Old Grey Whistle Test." They split up in 1977.

The individual members of Wally weren't too happy about the situation, some taking it worse than others. I'd met up with them post gig in the Roundhouse car park that was on a raised level above Chalk Farm Road. I think I was commiserating with Pete Cosker when the night was shattered by the sound of a large engine kicking into gear. We both turned around to see Pete Sage sat in the driving seat off a large caterpillar bulldozer. Somehow, God only knows how, he had managed to get the thing working and was gently chugging towards the wall of the car park and the vertical drop that led to Chalk Farm Road. Without thinking I raced after it, caught it up and leapt onto the moving caterpillar tracks. Someone else had the same idea and I was aware he was on the other side. I made a dive for anything that looked like a control. The person on the other side did the same. We pushed and we pulled at levers whilst all the while Pete was sat in the driving seat laughing and giggling and generally being no help whatsoever. One of us, or perhaps both of us, made something move and the machine shuddered to a stop a few yards from the wall. Pete hopped off and ran off. We shrugged and followed. I left them all to it as I went off in search of my lift back to Harrogate.

Although they didn't win Wally had been spotted by one of the judges, Bob Harris, the presenter of televisions Old Grey Whistle Test. He took an active interest in the band and negotiated a recording contract with Atlantic records and a management deal with Brian Lane, the manager of Yes. Along with Rick Wakeman, the former Yes keyboard player, he also arranged to produce their first album, the eponymous "Wally". However changes had to happen. Mike Smith was replaced on drums by Roger Narroway, and for their second album Valley Gardens released in 1975, Paul Garrett was replaced by Nick Glennie-Smith. By now Wally had become a fully professional touring band covering Britain, Japan and the USA, although their base remained Harrogate.

Whilst all these rock and roll shenanigans were going on I had undergone a number of career moves. I had left W.H. Smith and Sons and had attempted to be a professional artist, by selling my drawings. I had some success with a couple of Leeds galleries who liked my pen and ink drawings of the Victorian streets and back alleys, and had a couple of shows in Harrogate's Aquarius Gallery, at the back of the Crown Hotel. I had met up with another struggling Harrogate artist, a guy called Neil Simone. Somehow we managed to open a gallery together only not in Harrogate. It was in York. It was in a round tower half in, half out of the River

Ouse just by Lendal Bridge.

The place had an interesting history. In its time it had been a home of a leather worker, hence its old name of Barker Tower. It had been a mortuary, it had been the home of the ferryman prior to the building of Lendal Bridge, and since World War II the home to York Council's street cleaning equipment. Of course the fact it had been a mortuary fascinated us and prior to opening, we issued a press release claiming the place was haunted. Of course it was bollocks, we knew it and the press knew it, but then as now, the press never let bollocks get in the way of a good story. I sold my drawings of York whilst Neil sold his paintings. Although despite being on the main tourist run into York the visitors didn't seem to want to venture down from the walls and the bridge to look at what we were offering. We didn't sell much and in order to pay its rent we took on a window cleaning round back in Harrogate. We earned enough to keep it going, well we would have done if we hadn't established a card school with the proceeds.

When Stuart and Dave noticed that Neil and I were actually making money they asked if they could borrow the ladders and try to clean some windows themselves. We let them providing they didn't go anywhere near our round, after all we'd paid good money for it. They didn't and one Saturday they disappeared off complete with ladders, cloths, shammy leathers and buckets. They were back mid afternoon. Stuart wasn't happy and I'm not even sure the two of them were on speaking terms. Eventually the story came out. Dave didn't like heights so Stuart did the upstairs. Then whilst Dave was doing some downstairs windows round the back, he stood on top of a little hut. He had barely rubbed the shammy leather over the window pane when the roof of the little hut broke and he found himself thigh deep in a rabbit hutch. Even worse, the shock had killed the family pet rabbit. Cue screaming, crying child and very angry father. The pair of them never borrowed the ladders again.

It was around this time that Dave and I did another gig at Harrogate Theatre, but appeared at separate slots on the bill. This was due to me trying an experiment. Neil had a reel-to-reel tape recorder and we recorded some backing tracks to my poetry. We didn't compose anything, neither of us were musicians. We recorded sound, and snatches of records. I can't remember what we actually did with the exception of one poem that I performed to Frank Zappa's track ""America Drinks and Goes Home". It was different and I think it worked....I think, although I never repeated the experiment because I've never had a reel to reel tape recorder.

Then Neil discovered a certain unique style of painting, there's a name for it but I can't remember it. My own description is super realism with a surrealist twist, they are landscapes, only when you look closely they are landscapes within other paintings, or landscapes falling off the canvas. They proved incredibly successful. He had a one man show in a Harrogate Gallery and sold out. We closed our gallery and he concentrated on his painting, knowing there was a demand for what he was producing. His style is still in demand today. In the intervening years I shudder to think how many paintings he's sold. Today he runs his own very successful gallery based in Pateley Bridge. He's also produced a book of his paintings alongside the story of his career. I get a mention on page eight. He's got his return mention just here!

Anyway Neil went off to paint and I went off to make a living by periods of signing on the dole, being a door-to-door Bettawear brush salesman and cutting grass in Harrogate's famous Valley Gardens.

I still stuck at the drawing and was rewarded by receiving a commission from the Yorkshire Arts Association in conjunction with the National Coal Board to do a series of drawings of Yorkshire pits. It took me the best part of a year, at the end of which there would be an exhibition at the Cooper Gallery in Barnsley. So ever so often, between everything else, I'd disappear off to Barnsley, Leeds, or Doncaster and make my way to a series of pits where I'd do some sketching, take a lot of photographs and come back to Harrogate to complete the final drawings. During that year I met and chatted to a lot of miners and had the micky taken out of me on many occasions. I discovered never to walk through puddles of slurry, and that on the pecking order of job importance, an artist is at the end of a very long line. Every time I visited a mine I was impressed with the humour, the work ethic and the sheer tolerance and bravery of the blokes that went underground. Yes they were well paid and yes they were militant, but by God they deserved it. If I faced the danger that they faced on a daily basis I would be militant about safety and working conditions. Each time I went underground in that cage and descended into the depths I thought I was facing my end. The lack of air and the dust was literally breath taking and each time I returned to the surface I considered myself lucky to be alive. I spent some time in their small South Yorkshire communities, mainly in the local pubs, and they were good places to be. That's why to this day I hate Margaret Thatcher and her Conservative Party not only for closing the mines, but for destroying the mining families and their communities.

Anyway back to the plot. It was whilst doing one of these final pit drawings that I threw an artistic wobbler. For some reason I just couldn't draw a letter A. Let me explain. The drawing was a view of the pits surface buildings among which as a tall chimney. Down the length of this chimney were some letters spelling out a pre Nationalisation company name. One of these letters was an A and for some reason I just couldn't draw it accurately. The more I tried the more I couldn't get it right and the more I thought about it the more I realised that I just didn't really know how the letter form worked. Then it dawned on me. I needed more information. I gathered up my portfolio and marched out of the flat and down the street to Harrogate Art College. It was October so the new term was in full swing. I knocked at the office door and asked to see the head of the graphics department. An appointment was arranged for the following day where I was interviewed by the Head of Graphics, Doug Wales, and two lecturers on the course Mike Robson and Roy Burnett, both artists who knew some of the fringe members of the Wally community. They knew me as well, though not as an artist but through my poetry. I came out of that meeting with the offer of a three year course, under the title of Visual Communications, which as far as I remember was a year foundation and two years of graphics. The term was underway so as far as they were concerned I could start the following Monday. I did. It was a bit of a risk as I had no financial support, but I could apply for a grant. I had been a Harrogate rate tax payer for some years and as I was now 24 I was counted as a mature student, Those two things ensured that I got a grant. At last I had made it to art college, albeit five years late. Today, (in 2019) that probably just wouldn't happen, and that's sad, it's also a reflection on wrongness of austerity and the way the arts and grants have been downgraded.

I completed the work for the exhibition and it must have been six months later. Stuart and a friend drove myself, my parents and a couple of other friends to Barnsley for the preview. The work looked good, it was framed and hung neatly along the white walls of the gallery. After we arrived, and as I was being taken aside and led away to talk to people and explain the exhibition, I noticed Stuart and my father had disappeared. My mother fretted and quiet rightly. Just as the exhibition was about to receive its official opening they appeared at the back of the crowd. My dad was drunk, he'd taken Stuart on a tour of Barnsley pubs looking for the fabled Barnsley Bitter. As the exhibition was about coal mining, someone had arranged for an opening speech to be delivered by Arthur Scargill, who at the time was the President of the Yorkshire N.U.M.. As he grabbed my hand and called me "Artisan Brother" I distinctly heard my father, a lifelong Conservative, say the word "Bollocks!" very loudly.

Dave and I were still gigging and perhaps the best gig Krax ever did was at Leeds Polytechnic supporting our poetic heroes that had reformed themselves into a band called Grimms, the members of which came from the bands The Scaffold, The Liverpool Scene and the Bonzo Dog Band. It must have been in 1973, going on 1974. Due to the size of Grimms, and the various member's individual projects, the line-up was always flexible, but I think I'm right in saying the line-up we supported that night was – Roger McGough, Brian Pattern, Adrian Henri, Neil Innes, Andy Roberts, Michael Giles, John Gorman, Dave Richards, John Megginson, Zoot Money, Ollie Halsall. I also have a feeling that William Rushston might have been involved somewhere along the line. Two things stand out in my memory. The first being backstage watching a very large Adrian Henri carrying a crate of Newcastle Brown Ale dressed only in a pair of very tight bright blue nylon underpants. (Adrian Henri, not the crate of Newcastle Ale!). The second watching the poet Brian Pattern giving a drunken performance of his poetry as he leant against the speakers stacked on the front of the stage. Needless to say he toppled the lot off the stage. No one was hurt. To us it was all part of the fun, no matter how drunk, no matter how shambolic their performance, we had supported the poets that had inspired us to write and to perform our poetry in the first place. We had met our heroes and they were irresponsible drunks just like us.

Since Wally had disappeared from the Harrogate scene Dave and I hadn't done a lot of performing apart from the occasional appearance at the Harrogate Theatre. . However, one of the less auspicious, but memorable gigs took place at a pub in Huddersfield.

We were on a small, raised stage with the audience sat at tables directly in front of us. We were seated, with a small table between us for our poetry notes and drinks, and a shared microphone on a boom stand. This is a stand with an extendable arm which we found could be swivelled back and forth between us as we read, rather than having to hold a microphone and pass it between us.

This was great at first, as one of us could read and then simply push the stand which would swivel round to the other poet. It also looked really smooth and professional, as the recipient would just flip the head to bring the mic to face him. What we didn't realise was that as the stand swivelled, it got slightly looser and slightly lower each time. Thus, halfway through the set, it was given a good push and set off in a low, sweeping arc out over the front row table, connecting with the necks of the bottles on the table and propelling their contents onto the occupants of said table.

The two couples at the table leapt to their feet but not in time to avoid the two guys getting a trouserful of best bitter. Needless to say, they were not amused, and neither was the landlord, who rushed over to see what the commotion was. We were expecting to be ejected from the stage via the nearest window, but fortunately the guys weren't too soggy and after we bought them replacement drinks and apologised profusely, we continued the act with sheepish faces and a hand-held mic. Unfortunately, we felt obliged to buy them a second round, which wiped out our fee for the evening and not surprisingly we weren't offered a return booking. However, it did give a whole new, if damp, meaning to the concept of audience participation.

It was at one of our performances at the Harrogate Theatre that we were approached by the two male members of Pulse, Steve and Gar. They wanted to join up with Dave and myself and revive the Krax band. That was a bit of a shock to us both. We gave it due consideration. Did we want to go through all that again? Yes, you bet we bloody well did!

We arranged a couple of rehearsals and things clicked, then completely out of the blue someone from the past made contact. It was Dave Abrams from the Seacroft folk clubs days. I explained what was happening and he was in favour of joining and so he came across to join in the rehearsals. His material, being a mixture of solid traditional and contemporary folk fitted in perfectly. Now Krax mark2 was born with the new line up of – Steve Fallows, spoken word/poetry. Gar Sutton, guitarist and singer/songwriter, Dave Pruckner spoken word/poetry Dave Abrams folk singer/guitarist, Graham Rhodes, spoken word/poetry.

I can't remember our first gig or where it was. Thinking back it was probably at a small pub called The Greyhound, well out of Harrogate up towards Masham in a small, one house village called Wath, where Stuart and some other mates used to drink. It had a lot of advantages that pub. It was well out if the way, had a very lax attitude to people having a joint around the back and tended to ignore regulation closing times.

By now dope had become a regular part in all our lives (with the exception of Dave Abrams). It would be rude to mention the who's and how's and the what's and wherefores, but a close friend had a contact and could order the stuff by the ounce. I should also explain that back in the day we scored hash, it was Moroccan, sandy coloured or red, or Afgan Black, or some Pakistani stuff. Grass was a rarity. Sometimes someone would get their hands on some Thai sticks but they were both rare and expensive. In the mid seventies drugs were commonplace in Harrogate. The Times newspaper ran an article claiming that per capita Harrogate had the biggest drug problem than any town in Britain. Its publication coincided with one of Wally's rare appearances. They were playing a welcome home gig at the Harrogate Theatre and Paul Middleton read the article out to a cheering audience. The local police never forgave the band or the audience, for weeks every time any of us went out we were either followed or questioned. To this day I've no idea if the Times article was right or where they got their facts from, but it was probably true and it wasn't just dope. Acid was commonplace. It was rumoured it was coming directly out of Leeds University's Chemistry department. There was particularly strong type called pyramid acid, so called because it was three times as strong as the normal dose. Then there was one bloke I knew that used to get people to buy cough medicine for him and he used to distil morphine out of it. His flat was like a giant chemistry set.

There was also heroin, if you knew where to look. Unfortunately the latter had already claimed one victim in our circle. Rosie was a really nice guy. He originated in Goa and ended up in Harrogate, the reverse of the hippy trail. He was well known in the local music scene and was usually found in the audience at the Cock and Castle and other pub gigs. I knew him and his friend Dolly o chat to, to have a drink with and to have the occasional game of cards with. It was the morning after such a night when someone rang my flat. Rosie was dead, overdosed during the night. For a while the whole Harrogate "scene" felt the shockwaves, then as The Eagles once sang,-

"And we who must remain go on living just the same" Bernie Leadon. By the way, that lyric was written about Gram Parsons, another drugs victim.

I suppose this is the right place to write about drugs and my attitude to them. I always smoked roll-up cigarettes, because they were cheap, so I was always susceptible to rolling a joint. I liked dope. I always have and always will. I preferred it to alcohol. Given a choice I preferred being stoned to being drunk any day. It was more fun. Drunkards fight, stoned people laugh. I didn't like the feeling of being drunk, I didn't like the aggression alcohol brought out in me and in others. By now I could drink, I'd had a lot of practice and it took a lot to get me drunk, too much. I hated the bloated stomach feeling and I really hated the throwing-up. No, give me dope any time. You can get creative on dope, you get destructive on alcohol. Now as I write this in 2022 after suffering two heart attacks, I don't smoke, I don't take anything except the medically prescribed drugs which are as boring as hell, but necessary however, ironically, I still drink.

Back then I did flirt with acid. I found it useful. It provided a sort of springboard to my creativity. I maintain that acid opened up a few channels in my brain that, had I not taken it, might have been locked away and I might not have been such a good creative. I'm not claiming that acid created my creativity, but I am saying it helped, it sprang a few trapdoors in my brain. You have to be careful with acid. Make sure you're in a good place when you take it. Make sure you're in a comfortable and safe environment. Don't drop a tab and go off to the fun fair. I did! The dodgems and waltzer were ok but I freaked out at the top of the big wheel and tried, unsuccessfully, to climb out of the seat and move hand over hand across the scaffolding. The wheel started before I could get out and whoever was in the car with me dragged me back in and told me not to be a dickhead. That was my only bad experience and that was my own stupid fault. A good experience was the day the Pink Floyd album "The Dark Side of the Moon" came out. Wally were in town and a certain member of the band and myself fixed a record deck up to the bands PA in their rehearsal studio, then we dropped a tab of acid each and played the album. That was what you call an enlightened experience. A couple of us also used to go to the local cinema tripping. We'd always sit on the very back row, so no one could see us. I remember seeing Jaws in that state and when the shark appeared, jumping so much that I hit my head on the wall behind me. Some of us also dropped a tab and went to a showing of Stanley Kubrick's "2001 a Space Odyssey." Now that was an interesting experience.

Dave once took a tab of the pyramid acid and sat in front of a poster of Gollum for two straight days. When he came round he claimed he'd got an entirely new spin on "The Lord of The Rings" and claimed that Gollum was really a decent guy. I couldn't argue. I'd spent the two days trying to walk across the rush matting on the living room floor. It had turned into a field of barley and I was walking on top of the stalks waving in the winds. Once whilst we were tripping we looked out of our third floor flat windows to see the Lord Mayor of Harrogate drift by in a basket suspended from a balloon, which was a sight you didn't get to see every day. It turned out that he'd climbed into the basket for a publicity shot for the local paper and it had slipped its moorings and drifted off over the Stray. Another day a herd of elephants trooped passed. Yes the circus was in town and had pitched their tents on the Stray, just down the road from us.

Acid and dope were good enough for me. I was never tempted to go down the Class A route. For a start I have always hated needles. I was also a witness to the dangers of heavy drugs when

Pete Cosker became unstable and had to leave Wally. Everyone tried their very best to help him. However he succumbed and sadly died some years later.

Back to the plot. One advantage of the new Krax line up was that both Dave Abrams and Gar Sutton had cars and drove. Occasionally we would hire a van, or more often get Stuart to drive us. We had decided to aim our new act towards folk clubs, after all they had been good to me in my early days and Dave Abrams was still known on the circuit. Mind you, to be honest, we aimed our act anywhere we could get a gig, anywhere where they would have us!

So what was this act? Well it usually started with a Dave Abrams song that we all joined in with. Then either Dave or I would do a poem before Steve and Gar did a musically accompanied poem. Then Gar would sing one of his self written songs with Dave joining him on guitar, then a poem from Dave P, then one from me, then another accompanied poem from Steve, a song from Dave A. That would take us up to break time and then we'd do the whole thing again, only with different material of course. We'd finish with Dave A song that we all joined in with and for an encore did a bizarre version of the "White Cliffs of Dover."

The musical poetry bits were interesting as they were sort of narrative story-poems. Steve and Gar did one about travelling down to London or was it Scotland, perhaps it was both. Then Gar and I did one about hitch hiking from Harrogate to Hunmanby, (a village just below Scarborough on the Yorkshire coast). Unsurprisingly it was called "The Thumb to Hunmanby." I don't have a copy of the words, neither do I remember any of the lines, which is probably a good thing. Looking back perhaps they were a bit pretentious, but we seemed to get away with it, especially when Dave P would pop up next with a comedy poem that would have us and the audience laughing.

We did a gig up the A1 at a folk club in Bishop Auckland and arranged that we would hire a van and that Stuart would drive us up there. It was a memorable gig for two reasons, the first being that as we ended the gig, instead of finishing with our version of "White Cliffs of Dover" the organiser climbed onto the stage and told the audience we would lead the club with the singing of their traditional song "Cushie Butterfield". We looked at each other in horror. None of us knew a song called "Cushie Butterfield". I looked at the organiser.

"We don't know Cushie Butterfield!"

He looked back *"Of course you do."*

We all shook our heads. It seemed incompressible to him that anyone didn't know his clubs favourite song, but we didn't. Eventually he dragged various members of the club up onto the stage to perform the song as we five stood among them vainly and vaguely trying to sing the words to a song we never knew. Oh we all know it now. I think by the time we left that stage it had been drilled into us. It's the one that goes –

"She's a big lass
She's a bonny lass
And she likes her beer
And I call her Cushie Butterfield
And I wish she was here"

What made the thing even worse was that its one of those songs that has endless verses and goes on forever. Anyway we did it and no bones were broken. After the gig was over and the audience was leaving we looked around for Stuart. He hadn't been seen all night. We found him in another bar huddled with a group of locals. By the number of empty glasses in front of him I figured he'd managed to consume at least a dozen rum and blacks. He helped us load the van and we all piled in. It was a rocky trip back especially when he completely missed a roundabout and ploughed straight over it, across the road and the van stopped on the grass verge just as it was about to drop into a ditch. The people in the back, together with the gear, got thrown around a lot. No one said a word. Everyone was deep breathing, feeling lucky to be still in one piece. To break the silence I heard my own voice saying -

"Steady on, I've dropped the joint!" As it happened I had, and I was sure I could smell burning.

We also did a "Peoples Festival" in Leeds. It was in the open air on Woodhouse Moor near to the University in the middle of student land. That time it was just the three poets Dave, Steve and myself and we shared a very large joint before going on-stage. That we were stoned out of minds can be the only reason we thought that performing our set wearing clown make-up was a good idea! I've no idea where we got the make-up from but we mounted the stage wearing white faces, eye make-up and huge red lips. It was only when we stood on the stage that we realised there wasn't a P.A. No microphones, no speakers. Instead we were handed a megaphone. Just the one between the three of us! So we did the only thing we could do, each of us took our turn to shout our poems holding a poem in one hand and the megaphone in the other. Yes of course it sounded rubbish and yes it must have looked odd, even for the early 70's. I don't if any of the audience actually heard what we were saying but we got a smattering of applause after each poem, and a round of applause as we left the stage. As soon as we were out of sight we made straight for the public loos and washed the make-up off before we meandered back to the stage to watch the rest of the entertainments. As we sat on the grass I watched the guy who was acting as MC. As he handed the megaphone to someone else I noticed he had a large red mark all around his mouth. Then the person who had just spoken passed the megaphone back. He too had a large red mark around his mouth. It went on like that for at least three speakers before we decided to slip away unnoticed before anyone realised what had happened and who was responsible for smearing red lipstick all over the megaphone. The audience knew. After every speaker handed the megaphone back, certain people sat around us would smile and look towards us and nod. We chuckled about it all the way back to Harrogate.

This version of Krax was much more successful than the first. Again we played the Harrogate Theatre as part of Youth Theatre gigs, and as a part of the Harrogate International Festival Fringe. We played the bar, the studio theatre and the main theatre. At one gig we played the main stage and carefully arranged three wicker chairs for the three poets to sit in. I think we were going through a Somerset Maugham period. I've no idea where we found them, probably backstage somewhere. Anyway we placed them on the front of the stage and made sure the mics were set to us in a sitting position. Gar and Dave would then stand slightly behind us. It looked good in the rehearsal and it worked. The trouble was there was a lot of time to kill between rehearsal and the actual performance. Almost four hours, enough time for us to go back to the flat, get stoned, pop into the pub on the way back and have a couple of drinks or so. When we arrived back at the theatre, in good time I may add, we were shown to our dressing room that was right at the top of the building. We kept ourselves amused in there giggling and mucking about and laughing at some sort of little box on the wall that squawked and made strange gurgling noises as if someone was talking under water. It was a few minutes later that Dave Abrams, the only one who hadn't smoked, noticed that it sounded like it was saying "Krax!" We listened , we could just make out that we were wanted somewhere with five minutes to go. Someone looked at a watch and with a sobering dawning of reality, we realised we were due on-stage. We stumbled out of the dressing room and down goodness knows how many flights of stairs. They seemed to be going on forever until we found ourselves at the head of a short corridor and into the wings. where someone was standing ushering us directly onto the stage. We three poets sort of leapt on the stage, saw the chairs and made great strides to get to them. The only problem was that the three of us all made for the nearest one and found ourselves colliding in our haste to get sat down. We paused and looked at each other, confused until we worked out what was going on. Then we each found our designated chair and sat down. It was Dave that lifted up a knocked over microphone.

"Hello it's us again!" he said.

The audience, half of which were as stoned as us, understood, gave him a cheer and we got on with the gig.

Somehow we managed to get some college gigs. I think it was at a Salford University fresher's ball where we shared a dressing room with a snake charming, fire-eating stripper. (Oh come on it was the early seventies. It was the time when Bernard Manning hosted the Wheeltappers and Shunters Social Club on Saturday night television!). For most of the time the snake kept itself to itself in the dressing room. I can't say the same for the stripper. We didn't know where to look, I mean for God's sake she was a very attractive and well endowed woman. Then she offered to teach us how to eat fire. Well that was out for both me, Steve and

Dave Abrams, I mean the three of us wore beards. But Gar seemed up for it. He went into a huddle with her as she explained and showed him how to line his mouth with Vaseline. I'm not too sure he actually learnt the secrets. Put it this way it never appeared in the act.

We were in danger of becoming a serious band, We even had some publicity material made. One of which was a photograph, with me sat in the middle holding a Union Jack as the rest of them stood around me. I'm not too sure of who actually took the shot, but as I was at art college it was probably someone there. About ten years ago another photograph turned up. It was obviously from the same session as we were all wearing the same clothes, (Me in a River Island, velvet jacket for God sake!), only the positions were different we were all standing up holding a naked girl, that seemed to be sprawled among us. Honest it came as a right shock to me. I couldn't, and still can't remember a thing about it. I can't remember it being taken and I've no idea who the naked lady was. I'm not even sure I still have it. I arrived via email and I stored it somewhere but that was three computer crashes ago and in the days before I learnt to back everything up on external hard drives.

We also had a hand drawn poster that claimed "Krax eats schoolgirls!" I know these days it's so anti PC that it screams out, but again this was back in the day and it was a rip off from Adrian Henri and the Liverpool Scene. He was, and still is one of our favourite Liverpool poets. He seemed to write nothing but poems about falling in love with schoolgirls. In fairness so did Roger McGough, but Adrian Henri seemed to make a career out of it. Recently I listened to his two Liverpool Scene albums and realised just how much that band influenced Krax. In fact if we had have made a recording of us back then, it would have sounded just like them. It was all these years later that I realised what we had set out to achieve had already been done, and done a lot better.

I was around this time that Dave P. moved back to Leeds. He got himself a job and a flat on the top floor of a Victorian house in the Hyde Park area. We were now spread out as Steve and Gar shared a flat with their respective girlfriends Elspeth and Patrina in York, near enough to see the Minster. I was still in Harrogate and Dave Abrams was still living with his girlfriend Mary out in either Ilkley or Otley way. Sometimes we rehearsed at mine, and sometimes we rehearsed in York.

In actual fact the act didn't need very much rehearsal. Despite being a band we all did our own material. I did my poetry as a solo bit, so did Dave P, Steve's material was usually stand alone and sometimes accompanied by Gar strumming a guitar and Gars songs were stand alone, sometimes with Dave A strumming along. Dave A's songs were pretty stand alone, in fact they were the same songs he had sung at the Seacroft folk club, sometimes with Gar strumming along and sometimes we all joined in the choruses. But there was nothing in the act that required a deal of work or anything that was really musically complex. It was a lot of separate parts that when we put it together, sort of fitted into a long cohesive entertainment. Dave A didn't change his material much as he had an album out called "If I'd Stayed Around". I had done the sleeve, it was one of my black and white drawings of Whitby.

Usually a rehearsal would comprise a chat about the previous gig, what worked what didn't, then an attempt to fine tune it, then new ideas and finally we'd crack out the dope and smoke and jam and chat. One night we were rehearsing at Steve and Gars flat in York when a thunderstorm broke out. As we looked out of the window we could see the lightening flashing around the steeples and towers of York Minster. They had some acid and we all dropped a tab and spent the rest of the night watching the lightening dancing over the roofs of York whilst listening to Nico's "Marble Index" album.

The same line-up experienced another lightening incident on the way back from a gig at the country pub, near Wath that I mentioned earlier. It was in the early hours of the morning and we were all travelling in a van when a storm broke out. There wasn't much rain but a lot of lightening. In fact it was dancing along the road in front of us. Again we were in an altered state of mind and we got whoever it was doing the driving to stop the van and we all climbed up onto the roof where we sat and watched the lightening hitting the road in front of us. Whatever we were on we never stopped to even consider what we were doing was dangerous. We just sat there transfixed as the lightening popped and fizzed and crackled around us. It was both thrilling and scary, especially as we could actually smell the electricity in the air. Mind you we did get soaked.

There's one more drug related story to tell from this incarnation of Krax time. It concerns Dave P. It was coming up to the time for a rehearsal at his place. As we parted from a gig Steve mentioned the time and the date and added,

"Get some dope in, you never have any!"

To which Dave replied with his witty one liner. *"I do, I have most of yours!"*

When we all climbed off him and he scraped himself up off the floor we made arrangements for him to buy a full ounce. We even made arrangements of it to be delivered to him. The rehearsal was arranged for a Saturday, the delivery arranged for a Tuesday. On Wednesday I got a phone call from Dave.

"How do you roll a joint?" he asked.

"Do you have any papers and tobacco?" I asked.

"No!" was the reply.

"Well crumble some in your coffee!" I suggested.

Come Saturday Steve, Gar and myself were in Leeds ringing Dave's doorbell. There was no answer. We tried again and again. We shouted. Eventually a dishevelled head appeared three flights above us.

"Let us in." we shouted.

"What are you doing here?" he asked.

"It's Saturday. Its rehearsal time!" we shouted up.

There was a pause.

"What happened to Thursday and Friday?" came the answer.

He eventually come down and let us in. When we got to the flat it looked like a bomb had exploded. There were albums all over the place.

"Come on, roll up a joint." Steve said.

"I can't." Dave replied.

"Why?" we all asked.

"I've used it all." Was the reply.

"What!!!!" We exclaimed.

And he had. It turned out that we'd scored some particularly crumbly sort of Moroccan and when he came to crumble some in his coffee he didn't cut a bit off he just crumbled the big lump. Needless to say he crumbled the full ounce into the coffee

"What did you do?" We then asked, having more than an inkling of the answer.

"I drank it!" he replied.

How the hell he never suffered cannabis poisoning I'll never know. He looked around at the scattered albums and blinked.

"I think I had a good time!" He said.

The transport that we travelled to gigs in always had a tape deck and we'd argue about the music we'd play all the way to the gig, with one exception. It was the album by Dr Hook called "Bankrupt". We all loved that album, especially as we smoked that pre-joint gig to put us into the right head state, a sort of semi-stoned, comedy, good-time feeling for whatever the gig ahead might throw at us.

Not every audience liked what we did. We got paid off at the Processed Pea club at Etton, somewhere near Beverley. When we tried to protest we were told our humour was "Micky Mouse!" That upset a couple of the band and they jumped up and down in the flower tubs outside the pub. It didn't help the situation.

Separately Dave and I performed the Cock and Castle as Krax

and were there on a fateful night when the organiser Graham Cardy had a truly brilliantly insane idea. He tried an experiment and gave an instrument to the first five or six people who entered the place and got them up on the stage to play. It was musical mayhem, but oddly enough it sort of worked. He developed this idea over the following weeks until a rough and ready band began to emerge. They were christened "The Mirror Boys." It's difficult to describe what they sounded like, but let's try. How about a rough blues mixed with a series of chaotic chords and notes? There were tinges of Captain Beefheart, Zappa meets Stockhausen and Varese. It was odd probably to musical purists, unlistenable. At one point I won't say I actually managed them, but I got them bookings. It was always fun the morning after one of their gigs when the venue would ring me up to ask, *"What the fuck was that?"*

I even managed to negotiate then a support slot on the first ever Sex Pistols tour, but the gigs were cancelled. They had a connection with Wally, apart from The Cock and Castle, Paul Middleton's younger brother Phil played harmonica with them. They even played two or three gigs together. Once they topped the bill over Wally due to Roy Webber stating,

"There's no way I want to follow them!"

One gig was at Harrogate Art College. By now I was well established and was student union president, which actually sounded much grander that it was. We didn't have a student union room or even a student rest room, we usually used the nearby Coach and Horses pub, despite this Phil Middleton was student union entertainment manager. Hence most of the gigs (about two a year), would feature Krax, The Mirror Boys and sometimes Wally. Anyway this gig was going pretty well. Krax had opened up and we'd done our thing, The Mirror Boys were halfway through their set when suddenly for no reason whatsoever a student decided to hit his mate over the head with a pint glass. Somehow the police got involved and Phil and I ended up in the Harrogate Police Station with a puzzled College Principle wearing a coat over his pyjamas. I don't know if Wally got to play, but as the gig was being held in some Council owned building it got shut down, and Graham Cardy led the audience, pied piper like through Harrogate to a late night drinking establishment called The Wanderers where the party carried on well into the early hours.

I've no idea where it was but one gig we did was recorded. We used a port-a-studio owned by the art college. I remember editing it, but I've no idea where the finished cassette went to. A few years ago, around 2005 a CD turned up that contained some Krax performances, but for reasons best known to himself Gar had splattered dance music over it. I don't recommend listening to it. It certainly isn't representative of the material we were performing at the time.

Despite the drugs, the drink and the mayhem of live gigs, we were all serious about our material. Gar was a damned fine musician and song writer and spent a lot of time developing new songs and ideas. Dave Abram's was a very proficient folk singer with a wealth of good material up his sleeve. Steve was a good poet and writer and, well I've already told you how good Dave was/still is. I also stuck to the task. For me I've never found that sitting and straining to find a poem was a very productive pastime. I've always waited till a line or an idea landed in my head. Then I would sit down and try to tease it out, but the idea or line had to arrive first. Despite that I was pushing myself to write new and decent material. Of course we were each other's fiercest critics. Once a new bit of writing was completed it would get read out to the others for approval, and adjusted accordingly given the response. If no one liked it, it never got performed.

We did a gig at Otley Folk Club and halfway through the night Dave and I suddenly realised we couldn't get back home to Harrogate. Steve and Gar had brought their girlfriends and there was no room in their car. Dave Abrams was going in the opposite direction. Dave and I were stuck. In the middle of our second half I mentioned this state of affairs to the audience. Nothing happened. As we finished the gig and began our encore I mentioned it again. By now I was almost begging for someone to offer us a bed for the night. The gig ended and as we packed up and chatted to members of the audience I noticed a rather large and solidly built young lady elbowing her way through the people.

"I'll put you up!" she declared.

With that she almost dragged Dave and myself out of the pub, stuffed us into a mini, and drove off with us into the night. I've no idea where she drove us to but she eventually pulled up at a house and ushered us into the living room, where four more young ladies were sat watching TV. We were in a house shared by five nurses. I think I'll just leave it there, with the exception of saying she very kindly dropped us at the bus station the next morning.

For some reason on the folk club circuit there was always a tradition of being taken to someone's house before you can get off home. Once there you are offered drink and coffee and expected to do an extra performance. It happened to us on a number of occasions, but one such visit left me massively embarrassed. We were in someone's house, Dave Abrams was playing the guitar. The owners of the house had invited other people round so it was almost a party and we were the unpaid entertainment. In the middle of this I needed to go to the toilet. I slipped away and went upstairs. As I stood there I noticed the WC was the old fashioned sort, with a water cistern balanced above the loo on two brackets with a chain hanging down. I finished and pulled the chain. I must have pulled too hard because suddenly the cistern seemed to overturn and a couple of gallons of water tipped out all over me. I was soaked from head to foot. I panicked, well wouldn't you? I tried to find a towel and get the water off me. Then I noticed the water was still coming. I stood on the loo and tried to push the cistern back onto the two brackets. It wasn't easy but I eventually managed it. It didn't look right, the pipe leading up to it was horribly bent, and the big water cistern hung at a silly angle, but at least the water had stopped flowing. Once again I tried to dry myself off and wondered what to say to the householder. I rather hoped I could just sneak back into the room and get away with saying nothing. Not a chance. As soon as I opened the door Dave P was in the middle of one of his poems. He looked across at me and asked

"Why are you all wet?"

The entire roomful of people turned round to look at me. I did my best to explain but as I spoke I began not to believe the story myself. I sort of pointed up the stairs in the direction of the toilet and tried to explain, but failed. I was offered another coffee and the opportunity to dry off in the kitchen. We didn't stay much longer after that.

Krax came to an end in a quiet way. It was the morning after a gig at Bentham Arts Centre. We were sat around in a bed and breakfast place finishing our coffee when someone suggested we stop doing it, and we all simply agreed. There were no arguments, no musical differences, no traumas, we all just agreed it had come to a natural sort of end. Steve and Gar went back to York. Eventually Steve went travelling and Gar returned to Scotland,

Dave Abrams returned to the Pennines and became involved with education, Dave Pruckner went back to Leeds and worked for the council and never stopped writing, or being my friend. Although this was the end of the Krax band Dave continued working with Andy Robson on Krax Magazine until 2014. I went back to Harrogate and carried on doing what I was doing, little realising that I would soon experience some huge changes.

Back in Harrogate and in my final year at art college I did a couple of gigs by myself. One was at Ulverston Arts Centre, a gig that would have gone a lot better if I hadn't have been introduced to a local beer called Hartley's Bitter. I also did a gig in a York Arts centre that had been established in a church. For that one I supported the Mirror Boys, who by now, or on that night, were at least nine strong with one guy using a large enamel petrol advert as a wobble board.

During the Christmas break the art college put me up for a job. It was demonstrating products made by Cumberland Graphics at various trade fairs. Originally I did one in Harrogate at the International Toy Fair and they liked what I did and booked me to do two more. One in London and one in the NEC in Birmingham. Fine by me, it was good money. The only thing was they wanted me to use something they had just launched, something called Roller Art where you were expected to paint with different sized rollers, not brushes. The only thing I found I could paint was large industrial landscapes featuring cooling towers and angry grey clouds. Someone must have had a sense of humour because they kept me on. They also kept all the work I did for them. The trade fair in London was in Olympia and as I was down there for a week I got in touch with an acquaintance from Leeds who invited me to their flat in Finchley. I found my way there where he introduced me to a woman he shared the flat with. Her name was Jane and we fell in love immediately. She gave me a lift back to my hotel and we saw each other every night that week. When I returned to Harrogate I had no idea what to do. We kept in touch by phone and a bit later when I booked into the hotel in Birmingham there she was waiting for me.

At the time I was managing and operating the sound desk for a jazz, funk, rock band called Dancer. They were much younger than Wally, but decent enough musicians. I had a couple of ridiculous adventures with them. At a gig in Wakefield I was working the PA when a great big hairy hand reached over my shoulder and began playing with the master volume control. As it happened I was wearing a big brass bracelet that I still wear to this day. I slammed it down on the hand and by the crunch it made I knew I had caused some damage. It withdrew. Then before I knew what was happening a huge hand had me by the throat and lifted me off my feet. As I was now head and shoulders above the audience I caught the eye of the bouncers. Now I always believe in making friends with bouncers, and earlier, as the band were doing their sound check, I had made a point of chatting to the bouncers and buying them a drink. One was an ex-boxer who had severely injured someone in the ring and as a result had had lost his license, and the other was his punch drunk young prodigy. They saw my plight and pushed through the crowd, punched the man holding me who was a huge bloke, grabbed him and then ran him through the crowd and smashed him head first into the bar pumps. As he collapsed they grabbed him again and threw him through the pubs front doors. He didn't come back.

Then there was the time when the keyboard player, an intelligent idiot called Simon, thought it would be a good idea to drop a tab of acid just before going on-stage, with the result that I had to spend thirty minutes persuading him, in front of the audience, that he wasn't a tortoise and that he should come out from under his keyboard because there was a lot of very nice people just waiting for him to play his keyboard. Musicians!

One night we were coming back from a gig, dropping everyone off and there was just me and the sax player in the back of the van. We were chatting when he suddenly said he was thinking of leaving the band to go to Leeds College of Music and that he was also going to get his front teeth removed so he could play the saxophone better. I found myself admitting I was thinking of leaving Harrogate, leaving my wife and going to live in London. Within the month we both did what we promised each other. He went to Leeds and I went to London. As an after note the sax player made the right decision. Today he is known as Snake Davis and over the intervening years has experienced a brilliant musical career. Oddly enough we've never run into each other since that night in the back of the van.

Chapter Three - London
1977 - 1987

I separated from my wife and moved to London where I lived with Jane. At first I got some short term freelance graphic design jobs. Designing the Tupperware house magazine was probably the worse, designing book jackets for Octopus Books was the best but then, after meeting someone at a party, I was invited to work for an audi-visual company on the Goldhawk Road, in West London, an hour and a half's journey from Dukes Avenue, Finchley Central via the Northern and Metropolitan tube lines. A journey made even madder by travelling during rush hour. I didn't know much about audio-visual presentations, it turned out to be the projection of 35mm photographic slides in line with a pre-recorded audio tape. At first we thought it was cool linking three projectors to fade and dissolve using punch tape as a control mechanism, then the first computer came out of America. It was called a Spindler & Sauppe. It allowed the programmer to add pulses onto the audio tape that controlled the projectors. Now we could make six projectors not only fade and dissolve, but cut and create soft cuts. We then discovered that by linking two of these computers together we got a twelve projector show, and that was halfway to animation. I was working at the cutting edge of technology and discovered that when it came to design, there were no rules. It was exciting days.

At the same time I was getting involved with audio-visual design I got a phone call from Harrogate. It was from my old mates The Mirror Boys. Somehow they had got a gig at The Rock Garden in Covent Garden and wanted me to work the sound desk for them. I had no problems with this so on the appointed night I turned up and helped them set up. There were around six or seven of them and we sound checked and I did the sound for their set. I think they played for around forty five minutes and everything went smoothly. Just as their set was coming to an end I felt a tap on my shoulder. I turned round. There was a bloke there, smartly dressed with short hair. He spoke with an American accent. He explained that his band were on next but their sound engineer hadn't turned up and asked if I could do the sound for them. I nodded and asked what the line up was. Three piece, he replied, the singer likes a lot of reverb. I looked towards the stage as the Mirror Boys were finishing. No problem I said. So at the interval I helped the Mirror Boys pack up, waved them goodbye and settled down behind the sound desk once again. The following band was an energetic three piece playing a sort of punk rock with a slightly reggae feel to its beat. The audience had shrunk since the Mirror Boys and the only thing I noticed was that there was a woman dressed in a wedding dress, and as the band played their set she slowly took it off until she was half naked, and then she just walked away. The gig ended and I got invited to the backstage after gig party. It was some sort of going away party for a Hell's Angel called Goat who was on his way to jail. I found myself chatting to a man called Nick Jones who was part of the main bands management team. I told him I wasn't really a sound engineer but that I was a graphic designer. Hearing that the real manager, the guy who asked me to work sound, gave me his card and told me to call into his office. I popped in the next day and was taken onboard as a freelance graphic designer. The name of the band? Oh yes, they were called "The Police", it was their third ever gig. I ended up working with their management until 1982.

I would call into their office in Blenheim Terrace once or twice a week, around four or five o'clock where a brief would be waiting for me. Nick and his assistant, an American biker punk called Vermillion Sands, would be there to say what was wanted and when it was wanted by. Vermillion also fronted her own band, Vermillion and the Aces and proudly claimed she was president of the Nazi Motor Cycle Sluts, San Francisco Chapter.

There was very little actual design work to do, most of it was to mark-up art work for a printer, or to work out how something could be done. Back in those days a printer wouldn't accept art work unless it had a union sticker on it. I was a fully paid up union member and my sticker and union number went on every art work that left Step Forward Records. Once the work was handed over they would usually drag me off to some gig in town. Well it would have been churlish to refuse, especially as we always got in for free. Miles Copeland's name always assured guest list status. One thing about Miles was that he was very generous with back stage passes. Obviously many of the gigs were to see The Police, that was more or less compulsory, I think I saw them around thirty five times.

It's funny but looking back you can tell when a band is going to "make it". It's when the dressing room is full of strangers. At first the backstage crew were Nick, Miles, Vermillion, myself and the sound guy. By the time I left their company the band were ensconced in an inner dressing room protected by three layers of security with everyone and his dog milling around outside telling anyone who would listen (usually a bored security man) their connection with the band and how they were all there at the beginning and how Sting, or Stewart or Andy, would be so upset if they only knew that they, the speaker, were stuck outside.

Anyway all this is better described in my other book "The View from the Pink Monster" – my autobiography that chronicles life as a graphic designer and the street politics of London and what I got involved in. In that book, for whatever reason, I never mentioned my poetry. This book and this particular chapter, corrects that omission.

I think I'd been in London little over a year when Dave visited me and reminded me about poetry. I hadn't written anything for ages and hadn't performed since I left Harrogate. It's understandable, not only was I busy with two jobs I was also playing the proverbial Northern tourist visiting the West End, The City, and generally walking around wide-eyed. I was so in love with the London Underground that it took me six months before I realised I could actually walk from Oxford Circus to Tottenham Court Road!

It would be 1979 when I dug out my old act and considered performing again. I didn't want to go to a poetry club. I have never liked that type of place or the poetry that gets read there, and back then there were no stand-up venues, alternative comedy was yet to emerge. So I got hold of a copy of Time Out and checked out the folk club listings. Sure enough there was a club near to me. It was called the Orange Tree Folk Club, in the Orange Tree pub in Barnet. That was just up the road from Finchley, so one night I took my folder and went up. The organisers were a lady singer called Jill Darby and her partner, Ron Causton. They had no objections to a performing poet and so I got up and performed three poems. I've no idea what they were but they went down well and the organisers asked me back the following week. I had performed there about four times when I was approached by a singer who had performed earlier. He wanted me to join him and work as a duo. He thought my poetry would complement the material he sang. He was called Pete Smith and was tall, bearded and came from Birmingham. He used to sing a great song called "Plastic Pies" written by the Lancashire folk singer Bernard

Wrigley who I'd seen years previously at the Seacroft folk club.

Plastic Pies

Standing on the station at a quarter past eleven
Hadn't had a bite to eat since I got up at seven
Then I espies a tray of tater pies
So I went up to the bloke and ordered four
I shot back to the table 'cause my stomach was quite sore
But as I did I slipped and dropped the first pie on the floor
It hit the deck and caught me on the neck
Then it bounced back to the plate just like before

CHORUS: Plastic pies are all I see and all I ever get
Plastic pies and rubber cakes 'll polish me off yet
Well damn your eyes, and take your plastic pies
And you can shove 'em where the monkey shoves his nuts

I went back to the bloke and said "This pie's as hard as hell"
He looked the pie all over and said "This one's not been well"
He took off the crust and blew away the dust
Then said "I'll change the oil and the points and plugs as well"
I rushed back to the table where the first pie should have been
There were only crumbs upon the plate, and then I went quite green
It had crossed the floor, and walked out through the door
And it caught the half past twelve to Colwyn Bay

CHORUS: Plastic pies are all I see ...

An old man selling tortoises outside the pet shop door
A drunk came by and bought one then he come back for some more
He said "Ey up Jack" and clapped him on the back
And said "I've never had pies as good as this before"
Now prices they are rising fast 'cause no-one ever learns

And very soon we'll all see signs like 'Pies on Easy Terms'
90p a day would seem a lot to pay
When it's just for the deposit on the tray

LAST CHORUS: Plastic pies are all I see and all I ever get
Plastic pies and rubber cakes'll polish me off yet
Well damn your eyes, and take your plastic pies
And you can shove 'em where the monkey shoves his nuts
That's up his arsehole
Shove 'em where the monkey shoves his nuts
Recorded on ROUGH & WRIGLEY
Copyright Bernard Wrigley

We teamed up and played the Orange Tree regularly as a floor spot, then we began playing at another club called The Black Bull at Whetstone. It was there one night that we were joined by another singer, a thin faced, long haired young man called Mike Hurrey. He had performed solo for while but, like Pete, wanted to form a small group. Perhaps it was the need for strength in numbers. So now there were three of us, two singers with guitars and a poet who mumbled along with the choruses. We had a regular spot at both the Orange Tree and the Black Bull folk clubs and I became aware that there was a need to write new material, and so new material began to come.

We got a couple of actual gigs but mainly played floor spots, and then somehow, we got ourselves booked at The Talk of the Town, *THE* Talk of the Town, the famous London night club, the one on Charing Cross Road, the one where all the major stars of the fifties and sixties played. How the hell we got that gig I'll never know although it was a Sunday and it was a charity do, and we weren't the only performers. But even so, the three of us were standing on a stage that had been walked on by the likes of Danny

La Rue, Petula Clark, Eartha Kitt, Shirley Bassey, Liza Minelli, and Judy Garland. The list goes on and on. We were even given a dressing room in which we found a huge painting by Rolf Harris that filled one entire wall. He'd done it when he was performing there for a week, in the early seventies. I know it all turned out a bit sleezy for him when he got a jail sentence and there's really no excuse for what he did, however I do have to say he was a bloody dab hand given a wide paint brush and a can of paint.

Throughout my entire poetry "career" I've never put pressure myself to write my poetry. There's always been so much other stuff going on in my life that demanded my time, that challenged or entertained me. For me poetry would come as and when it chose to appear. It also used to appear when I was annoyed or angry, and the one thing that angered and annoyed me was the political situation in the mid to late seventies. Through my involvement with other projects and my introduction to Rock Against Racism I was growing more and more politically aware and felt the need to have a voice. Poetry gave me that voice. Actually I don't think it's a mystery to me that my most creative writing periods have occurred during the times of a Conservative Government. It was in 1979 when Thatcher rose to become Prime Minister, and the new religion of Thatcherism was born with its "greed is good" mentality. In my mind she was and still is pure evil, I knew that, Hell, I was living in her Finchley constituency. The woman was my M.P!

Back then the National Front were gaining strength, the previous year, wearing my RAR arm band I had worked with the punk band Sham 69 at six RAR gigs. I had also helped man the security and look after The Clash at their famous Victoria Park gig in Hackney. In the larger political sphere strikes were commonplace, and justified. The dustman's strike was in full swing. Leicester Square was overflowing with black bin liners, rats were scurrying everywhere.

On the musical scene the first wave of punk was giving way to something called new wave. A whole draft of new artists were emerging, wordsmiths like Elvis Costello, Ian Dury, Difford & Tillbrook of Squeeze, (who were managed by Miles Copeland and for whom I did some art-work), and of course the bloke I would be compared to for the next forty years, John Cooper Clarke. Being compared with him is no problem for me. I think his work is amazing. I'm a huge fan. His wit and word play is stunning and his first album was sheer brilliance. I especially love his poems "Kung Fu" and "Majorca". He wrote like I did, sweary stuff in everyday language. It was his emergence that spurred me onto not only performing again but to strive to raise my own standard of writing.

A poem I wrote around this time is the poem I still finish my act with today. It's called "Excitable Sadie", and there's a long story behind its conception. As I've already said I was freelancing for Miles Copeland and his stable of bands and I was backstage at an early Police gig. It would have been the summer of 1978 and I was with Nick Jones, and Vermillion Sands. The Police had done their thing and we were all sitting around chatting, chilling and drinking their gig rider when Andy Summers suddenly announced he was having trouble writing a poem about an inflatable doll. It was for a track on their first album which they were in the process of recording. We all laughed and chucked a few lines around, making a few suggestions before the conversation drifted onto something else.

As it happened the following weekend a Geordie friend of mine, Ned Smith was passing through London on his way to see Bob Dylan at his gig at Blackbush. Now I had experienced visits from Ned before, when I lived in Harrogate and I knew full well the only thing to do was to clear your diary and cancel all plans for however long he decided to stay. I had a number of lost weekends due to that man. I wasn't disappointed. He arrived with an ounce of grass, an ounce of hashish, a few tabs of acid and some speed. He might even have had a bit of coke with him. I did lose time, about a week I think. To this day I'm not sure if I went to Blackbush with him. I only have a few flashes of memory. One is of him haggling with someone on a train about the price of some sulphate, another is of a little figure in a hat, standing on a stage far away in the distance. Whether that was Dylan at Blackbush or not, I simply can't remember. Ned's visits had that effect on you. It was while he was on this visit that one night I mentioned Andy Summers and his search for an inflatable lady. We were on the floor at the time, rolling around giggling and the idea and the name "Excitable Sadie" cropped up. We tried to write it and we both added lines. Days after he left I found the tatty bit of paper and tidied it the writing up a bit and "Excitable Sadie" appeared. A week later I showed it to Andy Summers. He laughed but told me he'd already written one himself. That's the one that appears on the second side of The Police's first album which came out in the November of that year. Anyway as Nick pointed out, Miles would never have approved of mine going on the album as it would complicate the royalty payments. However over the years Sadie has worked well for me, and here she is -

Excitable Sadie
Excitable Sadie,
the inflatable lady
arrived through the post yesterday
so I undid the wrapping
and pulled out the packing
and took her upstairs to play.

I pumped and I pumped

and on her I jumped
I ran my hand through her hair
but I got my watch caught
and pulled her hair taught
and out came a fountain of air.

Well, she let out a fizz
and started to whizz
and shot round and round in the room
she startled the cat
when she shot passed the mat
and out of the window she zoomed

So It's goodbye Sadie,
the inflatable lady
the woman I've wanted so long
cos all I've got left
is a bit of left breast
with a label that say's Made in Hong Kong.
Graham Rhodes

Bless her, she's now over forty years old and I still end my act with her today.

Meanwhile up at the Orange Tree Pete suddenly announced he was leaving, not just our little trio, but he was leaving London to go back to the Midlands. Mike suggested that a bloke called Doug was interested in joining the band. What he failed to mention, until we met him, was that Doug was a bass player. He was one of the grumpiest people I've ever met. Later when we played gigs he would stalk up and down behind us and deliver a sharp kick in the back of the leg to anyone who dared to sing out of tune. Just what we didn't need, but he was a good bloke and could play the bass and he kept Mike in line, so now we were three again. Vocals and acoustic guitar, bass, and a poet! It was about then that the issue of a name cropped up. We were at the Black Bull Folk Club when the person introducing us asked what we were called. Without even thinking I looked up and said "Arkwright's Ferret." I've no idea where it came from other than I might have been watching TV and seen the John Smiths commercial of Arkwright drinking his John Smith's Bitter in a pub called The Three Ferrets. But the name stuck. From now on Arkwright's Ferret was going to be a major player on the London folk scene. It's just that the London folk scene didn't know it yet!

Obviously the band needed someone else, a guitarist and, as luck would have it there was also a vacancy for a graphic designer at the audio visual company I was working for. I had an idea and I made a phone call. I was still in touch with people back in Harrogate and Stuart had informed me that my ex-wife Ruth had rented out a room in the flat to young man who I had been to art college with. His name was Chris Dring and he was originally from Leeds. He played guitar and he was a decent finished artist. I had a word with the studio head, a mad New Zealander by the name of Fred Tunnicliffe. He was actually a glass designer who had come to England to work for some glass company but by accident, found himself in the world of audio visual. He swore a lot with the most creative swearing and cursing I've ever come across. His vocabulary was a wonder to listen to. If anything went fast it went –

"faster than a quart at a wharfies picnic".

If a bit of artwork was not straight it was –

"all over the place like mad woman's shit!"

He once was so sick of the studio phone ringing that he picked it up and threw it out of the window, which was closed at the time. He was entertaining to work with. He trusted my judgement and agreed to Chris working in the studio. Within a month he arrived in London, moved into a spare room in the house that Jane and I shared, found a place behind a drawing board at the audio visual studio, and played along with us at the Orange Tree Folk Club. Now the Ferrets were four.

Then Fang entered our lives. It's difficult to describe Fang. A writer for the Melody Maker once described him as "a man on his way to audition for the part of Robinson Crusoe". He usually wore a pair of battered trainers, camouflage trousers, a tatty tee-shirt over which was some sort of striped shirt over which was a large and very hairy, no-sleeved sort of body warmer thing. His hair hung long down to his shoulders and, the thing that gave him his nickname, wore a beard that was long and pointed and hung down below his chest. If you looked at his face you would see a pair of eyes twinkling behind a pair of round glasses. Not only was Fang an original but he was outrageous, as was his sense of humour. His vocal range was stunning, at times he sounded like John Martyn, and he could play the guitar almost as proficiently as John Martyn. In fact he performed a couple of John Martyn numbers and it was difficult to tell the difference between Fang and the real thing. Fang brought an entirely new dimension to the band, musically and visually.

We found a rehearsal space in the cellar of a building in East Finchley right opposite a real ale pub called The Windsor Castle. The building was some sort of office for the local council so there were no neighbours. We could make as much noise as we wanted. So now Arkwright's Ferrets were Mike Hurrey, Chris Dring, Fang, Doug and myself on poetry. We still did floor spots at the Black

Bull and the Orange Tree but we knew we wanted more. Then out of the blue we were joined by a keyboard player. John Laskey had been playing with another local folk group called Dumplings and Custard, but wanted a bit more challenging band to play with. We were certainly that. He turned up at rehearsals with a Prophet Five synthesiser that created a whole heap of new sounds. We were now one of the most unusual folk groups around. Now the new line up was a synthesiser played by John who was influenced by Genesis, Fang, a singer guitarist who pushed his acoustic guitar through a flange pedal and an old Marshal valve amp and who sounded like John Martyn. Doug, who bullied us into trying harder and who laid down a strong bass riff. Chris Dring who played electric guitar and was influenced by Kiss. Mike Hurrey who was more of a traditional type of folk singer, and myself rattling a tambourine, trying my best to do some harmony singing and performing poetry between musical numbers.

We eventually emerged from rehearsals with a set that included a number of traditional folk songs spiced up with a rock feel, some jokey acappella numbers, a couple of my poems that the band put music to, and a couple of numbers suitable for surprise encores. They were The Monkees "I'm a Believer" and Doris Day's "Deadwood Stage." I think the word to describe the set list is eclectic.

I can't actually remember where we performed our first few gigs, but they were mainly support gigs at folk clubs who had a bigger name on top of the bill. One of the first people we supported was a Londoner called John Foreman. He sang a variety of old music hall songs and folk songs and, between numbers as he was chatting to the audience, he would rip an old newspaper apart. Then as he finished his act he opened up the newspaper and revealed he had torn out a complete ships wheel. It was brilliant. It turned out he was the father of Chris Foreman, a young man who was making it big as a member of Madness.

We played support to another act that I was a huge fan of. It was at the Hampstead Folk Club and it was supporting the one and only Jake Thackray. I've enjoyed the man's songs ever since seeing him at the Seacroft Folk club and later on Bernard Braden's TV programme, a precursor to Esther Ranzen's "That's Life", way back in the 60's. I also remembered him from before that, when he was a teacher in Leeds because he taught someone I knew at Intake school. I managed to have a chat with him before the evening began. It wasn't about his songs, or his music. It was about Leeds and the various schools in the city. He laughed when I told him I was educated at Temple Moor, and we both scoffed at Foxwood. He couldn't remember playing the Seacroft gig.

I'm not sure if you have ever heard of Jake Thackray. If you haven't you really should check him out. Not only has the man written some of the funniest songs ever, songs like "The Castleford Ladies Magic Circle", or "Bantam Cock" or "Sister Josephine", but he has also written some of the saddest and most poignant songs like "Old Molly Metcalfe" "The Little Black Foal." Not only are his songs lyrically brilliant, but they were musically different to anything else on the folk club circuit. This was because in the very early nineteen sixties he travelled and spent time teaching English in France where he learnt the *chansonnier* tradition and became influenced by the work of Georges Brassens. Think Serge Gainsberg or Jaques Brel. That's why he style of singing and playing is different. He even included "Mr Gorilla", a French chansonnier song in his act.

It's funny how life goes around. Many years later, when I was living in Scarborough I met the man who still looks after my website, a Scot named Gordon Tennant. He was a member of the

Jake Thackray fan club who pressurised the BBC until they released their footage of Jake and was therefore responsible for the release of a much needed Jake Thackray DVD. Treat yourself to it.

I have a feeling that Jake never really liked performing. That he was never completely at home on the stage. When you look closely at the footage he always looks on edge. He was like that the night he played the Hampstead Folk Club. I've no idea what he thought of us, or what he thought of my poetry as he didn't see us. He disappeared before the evening began only to reappear a few minutes before he was due on stage and left quickly after his performance. .

Some clubs, mainly the bigger ones, insisted you played support slots before they would give you the top of the bill spot. The folk club in St Martin's in the Field was like that. We played there three or four times before they gave us the top of the bill spot. The club was in the crypt of the church that stands in Trafalgar Square. That excited me no end. I mean I was, and still am, a proud professional Northerner. Even though I'd lived there for a few years now I was still impressed when I came across the famous monuments and London landmarks. I also got a huge buzz out of seeing not so famous landmarks. Places like the Pie and Mash shop on the Goldhawk Road where it was said The Who used to meet in their very early days. I also got a buzz out of visiting the famous rock venues as a part of Step Forward records and the Miles Copeland entourage. I regularly visited the Hope and Anchor where I once saw an unsigned young ska band playing to a roomful of Crombie Boys dressed in coats and pork pie hats. It was Madness playing one of their very early gigs. I also saw the Pogues before they were signed, playing in a pub in Kilburn where the punks went mad to the Celtic punk rock, pogoing as they smashed themselves over the head with metal beer trays. It was through Miles Copeland that I found myself in the green rooms at both The

Rainbow and The Hammersmith Odeon. Of course I was impressed and got a thrill out of seeing famous London landmarks, which takes us back to St Martin's in the Fields.

The club was on a Sunday night and as I've said, we played three or four support spots before we eventually got a headline gig there. The odd thing about the club was that as you entered to set up your gear, the place always stank of boiled rice. I eventually discovered why. In the afternoon the crypt was a canteen for a Chinese Christian group who used to cook and supply food for the rest of the Chinese London community and for London's less fortunate. It was at that club where I came across one of the most difficult audiences I'd ever experienced. We were in our usual positions on the stage and the music was going down great. However when I performed my poetry I was aware that in front of me were about thirty women who just looked blankly at me. I tried everything to break through to them, to at least get a smile. The rest of the audience were fine, they laughed in the right places and gave the appropriate responses every time I finished a poem. It was just those thirty or so women. Not even a grin. I was beginning to wonder if every time I opened my mouth I was offending them. At our half time break I mentioned this to the organiser. He looked puzzled for a moment and then started to laugh. It turned out that the women were a group of foreign tourists who didn't speak English. The poor sods! They must have wondered just what was going on. They liked the music but every so often this bloke kept shouting words at them and looking more and more desperate every time he did it. In the second half of the show much to my own and their relief I moved to the opposite side of the stage where I could see the smiles and reactions to my poetry. The foreign tourists did stand up and sing along to our encore, which is probably more a testament to the enduring power of Doris Day than it was to Arkwright's Ferret.

The organiser of The Crypt was very supportive of the band and what we were trying to achieve. He wrote one of our first reviews.

"Just a quick note to thank you for the great night Arkwright's Ferret gave us recently. I think the band has a great future, and would recommend any club organiser who wants to give his audience value for money gets in touch with you quick! Please feel free to use me or the Crypt as a reference."
Graham Morrison, organiser The Crypt Folk Club St Martin-in the-Fields

I suppose this is the time to describe just what material Arkwright's Ferret were performing and what sort of act we had evolved into. We would start a gig with a traditional folk song giving it the powerful Ferret electronic rock style. It was usually a song called "Our Captain Cried All Hands", which started off with just voices and then built instrument by instrument until it rocked along. That would then merge into an electronic treatment of a traditional song called "Bonnie Light Horseman." Then another song sung acapella, that featured our harmonies, something like "Ilkley Moor Bah Tat" sung to the tune of "Amazing Grace". That would be sung with us wearing false rubber monster hands and sticking a finger in the ear. Then time for a poem. Usually it would be "Unemployment Poem" which led straight into our version of the traditional song "Blackleg Miner". Then Mike would usually sing a ballad, I would perform another poem and then we'd do a cover of Tom Lehrer's song "Masochism Tango", then it was time for a break. Of course between numbers there was a lot of banter and ad-libs between us and the audience as well as between ourselves.

The second half would begin with "Broom Besoms" a

traditional song that started off unaccompanied and ended up rocking. This was followed by a naval song called "Farewell Parker" that we added hand actions to and encouraged the audience to join in. That always got a great laugh.

We also did a cover version of Roy Harper's "When An Old Cricketer Leaves The Crease!" Then a poem of mine called "Space Invaders", more of which later. As encores we performed punk rock versions of Doris Days "The Deadwood Stage" and/or a version of "I'm a Believer" by the Monkees, but our version was much more like the Robert Wyatt version.

There was another number we did at the start of the Ferrets but for some reason, as we got more and more gigs, Fang didn't want to do anymore so it was eventually dropped. It was one of his own compositions called "Aging Heads". It can only be described as a psychedelic folk rocker. It built and built and at the end Fang used to holler, scream and shout whilst the band played louder and wilder. Chris used to let go some screaming guitar breaks whilst John played Pink Floyd like chords and swirls on the keyboards. Mike played chords on his acoustic guitar as Fangs flange pedal worked overtime. Doug held the whole thing together with a pounding bass line. I just rattled the tambourine. At one point it was the high point of the act. Why Fang fell out with it I'll never know, only that I know performing it took a lot out of him, which was why, when we did it, we usually ended the first half of the show with it.

Ageing Heads
Ageing heads wear five leaf earings
They roll all day, and occasionally snort lines
They don't work, they abuse their bodies
They take drugs that screw the mind.

Ageing heads say "wow far out man"
They don't appear to make much sense
They waste their lives philosophising
Their incomprehensibility is intense

They remember the sixties
As the halcyon days
Reminisce about peace and love
Through a post acidic haze

Ageing heads wear Woolworths flip flops
Grubby t-shirts and patched up jeans
They're untidy, they're unkempt
They don't know what haircut means

Ah but ageing heads are beautiful people
They believe in making love not war
They put flowers down rifle barrels
They believe that violence is a whore

They remember the sixties
As the halcyon days
Jefferson's "White Rabbit"
And Jimi's "Purple Haze"

Well you'd better not listen to what they say
They might put strange ideas inside your head
Like it's better to shoot yourself with horse
Than shoot somebody else with lead

Ageing heads wear five leaf earrings
They roll all day and occasionally snort lines…
Fang.

It was also around this time that we began to introduce some visual elements into our act. The most visual being a large tub of bright blue gunge that we threatened the audience with, of course it usually ended up being tipped over either Fang or Mike, and even then we contrived to make most of it miss. We soon got bored of it though and it didn't last long We had already introduced the monster hands when we sang unaccompanied. In the front line Fang, me and Mike would slide them on, hold them behind our backs and at a given point in the song would bring them up and hold a finger in our ears, thus taking the proverbial piss of the phrase "finger in your ear folk singing". The audience always got the joke.

Another innovation occurred one night, in the middle of a gig when Mike was singing. Halfway through the song Fang produced a carrier bag full of sponge balls. In a stage whisper he asked if I could juggle. I shook my head. Neither can I he replied, and proceeded to take the balls out and make an attempt. I followed suit and of course, as you might expect, we dropped the balls. We let them bounce away and took another three each, and dropped them. Of course the balls trickled off the stage and dropped into the audience. The audience threw them back. Then we threw them back at the audience. Now this was even funnier when you realise that Mike always sang with his eyes closed. As he ended the song he opened his eyes to see coloured balls whizzing backwards and forwards around him. Despite the fact that not one had hit him he wasn't very amused. But we kept it in the act, not every night , but occasionally, just to keep him on his toes.

Another visual that we used to do was towards the end of the act. To this day I've no idea how we got away with it or even if it was good idea. Looking back it just seems gross!

It was during a song called "It's Just Love!" written by Fang. It was a real schmaltzy love song that had John and his Prophet Five playing sweeping strings. It sounded like pure romance, until you listened to the lyrics. Whilst not obscene they were sexually deviant. *"You bite my buttocks and I'll lose my grip!"* was just one line.

Everyone would join in on the chorus of *"It's just love, ooooh!"* including myself.

In the meanwhile, during the break, I'd hidden a small glass of milk behind the monitor in front on me. Then, when everyone was looking at Fang I'd sneak a quick mouthful and hold it in. On the next verse I'd rub the microphone in a suggestive way finally sliding it up and down faster and faster in a masturbatory manner. Then, at the end of the final chorus, I'd breath very heavily and spit out the milk as if it was an orgasm. It usually went into the second or third row of the audience. Again, looking back now it seems bloody revolting. If someone gobbed milk all over me at a gig I'd be furious. But it was the seventies. Gobbing was still happening at punk gigs. King Kurt (a punk rockabilly band) were throwing offal at their audiences. Our audience loved it. Regular Ferret fans, and by now they were growing in their number, would stand in front of me and as the milk headed in their direction move deftly to one side. We recorded the song and it ended up being played on the radio, just the once.

In the 1990's I reworked it, changed the lyrics and gave it a whole new political ending. It's still in my act today, only it's not called "It's Just Love!" It's now called "Perversions".

Perversions
Draw closed the curtains

turn off the light
turn off the telly
and we'll do it tonight

You wear the pac-a-mac
I'll be the Nun
slide on your wellies
and we'll have some fun

It's nothing perverted
It's nothing strange
because you like bondage
don't mean your deranged

You bite my buttocks
and I'll lose my grip
I'll lay in chains
while you use the whip

We'll go to a place
where nobody goes
you sit on the bidet
while I suck your toes

I'll paint all of my
private parts red
while you wear my underwear
over your head

Your pour the treacle
and I'll lick it off
you hold my bits
while I have a cough

There's nothing perverted
it's really cool
cos I learnt these ways
from my old public school

There's nothing scary
There's nothing sinister
It's just a day in the life
of a cabinet minister.
Fang & Graham Rhodes

With material like this we began to attract reviews and attention within the folk scene. One critic described us as *"Steeleye Span meets Motorhead, and loses."*

In the summer of 1980, Thursday 10th July to be precise, we topped the bill at a thing called Folk in The Park. It was held in Victoria Park Finchley, virtually at the end of our road and part of the annual Finchley Festival. The bill comprised performers from both the Orange Tree and Black Bull folk clubs. It comprised Arkwright's Ferret, Dumplings and Custard, Tom Gilmure, Ron Causton and Jill Darby and was introduced by one Dave Pruckner!

As I've already mentioned, by that time I was involved in a small way with the anti racist organisation called Rock Against Racism and had written a poem called "I Want to be a Nation Front Skinhead!" It was satirical of course, but it was hard hitting. Halfway through our set I performed the poem and noticed that at the back of the audience there were one or two NF skinheads actually pogoing to it. Then as I continued speaking the words the penny dropped. I wasn't praising them, I was taking the piss. I carried on reading the poem as they began stomping towards the stage. Behind me I heard a member of the band say "I'm off!" Then as they reached the stage we all realised something that altered the entire dynamics of the situation. I was about five feet higher than them, and I had a microphone stand in my hand. I lifted the stand and dropped it on the head of one of them. Then I hit another. For a minute it was turning into a game of "Whack-amole". Then they decided they didn't like being hit over the head and left the tent hurling insults and threats. I got a round of applause from the audience and thanked God that they didn't return.

That November we decided to find out how popular we were. We were playing more and more headline gigs and no longer playing many support spots. We were playing folk clubs South of London, in places such as Sevenoakes, Bracknell, and Croydon, and in North London in places like Harlow and Bishop Stortford, we were building up a solid following. We knew we had a following in London itself, and we were getting positive mentions in folk magazines, especially one called Kasebook edited by a lady called Sue Duff who really understood what we were about and what we trying to do. She also enjoyed the fact that we never seemed to take ourselves seriously. At least that was the impression we gave. It was very different in rehearsals. There was the constant questioning of material, a constant pressure on myself to get gigs and keep the thing rolling. Because of members' work commitments there was the constant dilemma of not being able to book all the gigs we needed to be financially viable. We couldn't turn professional because there simply wasn't enough cash. It's still a problem for upcoming bands today, especially given the growing lack of places to play. Anyway we decided to find out just how popular we were and so we held the first Arkwright's Ferret Birthday Bash. We hired a venue in North London, printed up a load of tickets and posters and fly posted them all over London. We also put adverts in the New Musical Express, The Melody Maker, Time Out and Kasebook. We got a couple of folk acts to support us and then sat back and let it happen. We didn't sell out, but we didn't lose money.

On a winter's night in the first week of December 1980 we

played an out of town gig and myself, Fang, Mike, and Chris arrived back at Dukes Avenue in the early hours of the morning. Jane opened the door for us. She had been crying. As we trooped inside she broke the news to us that John Lennon had been shot. It hit us hard. We had all grown up with the Beatles. Occasionally we would cover "Working Class Hero". We sat around in a sort of daze, smoking and drinking coffee, each of us lost in our own thoughts, until one by one we drifted off to get some much needed sleep.

On January 8th 1981 Arkwright's Ferret made the front page of the local newspaper The Finchley Times complete with a photograph of us all looking very pissed off.

Here's what it said.-

Police's rock record

Dejected rock group Arkwright's Ferret had reason to look glum. When this picture was taken a sneaky thief had almost put paid to their plans for the big time. A guitar and irreplaceable sheet music had been stolen from the back seat of a car outside the home of one of the group in Dukes Avenue Finchley and with two gigs and a recording for its first single this week, things looked bleak.

However the story had a happy ending. On Monday Golders Green Police rang the group to say they had recovered the car which had run out of petrol in a Finchley street.

Singer Graham Rhodes, a graphic designer who lives in Dukes Avenue Finchley explained that the guitar, a 20 year old six string Harmony Sovereign Jumbo was on the back seat of a car belonging to group member Fang (Mark Rolf). He said the police have really been amazing to find it in such a short spaced of time must be a record. The guitar is so rare the guy could have destroyed it, but there wasn't a scratch on it. The group is sifting through the music to see what remains. Still missing is a flange – a foot pedal which distorts the sound and which costs over £100.

The members pictured above played last night at Jacksons Lane Community Centre in Highgate, tonight at the Black Bull in Whetstone, and on Saturday record their first single Space Invaders.

It's interesting that John isn't in the photograph. This could be that just after he joined the band he went into hospital to have some of his jaw removed. When he came out the lower part of his face was wired up and covered with a sort of wire mask. He looked like he was an American Football player. This meant that he could neither speak nor eat. For the first year he was in the band he communicated by grunts and bits of post it notes and ate by drinking lots of Complan through a straw. It's possible that at the time the photograph was taken he was in hospital, at work, or just didn't want to be photographed.

The article is a bit confusing as at first it reads that someone pinched Fangs guitar, flange unit and sheet music. It's only in the second paragraph that we find out that his car had been pinched as well when it mentions that the police have found the car! Not that the two events were related but it was shortly after this incident with his car that Fang moved into Dukes Avenue, living in a tiny room up in the attic.

The recording the article speaks of was done at a local studio based in Barnet. It was called "Weemeenit" and it was run by Steve and Edgar Broughton, the two brothers who were respectively the drummer and lead singer of the Edgar Broughton

Band, who became famous in the late sixties. I'd seen them a number of times and owned three or four of their albums. They were one of the more self-promoted hippy bands and experienced a small hit with a song called "Out Demons Out", which they played live as a long drawn out jam with the band and their idiot dancing audience chanting the phrase "Out Demons Out." They were also famous for staging free concerts and playing from the back of lorries.

Anyway due to everyone's work commitments we had booked ourselves in for a Saturday session, from lunch time to the late evening, possibly a twelve hour session. When we arrived we were met by Steve Broughton who booked us in at a reception desk where there were a line of glass jars full of illicit substances. We were told to help ourselves. There was grass, speed and I think, some coke. Then we were shown into a "studio" that looked like it was a cellar, lined with green flock wallpaper. It was only when we dragged our equipment into the room that I realised it wasn't wall paper at all, it was actually moss growing in the damp. Well the studio was the cheapest we could find, and was all we could afford. We knew we weren't there to make an album, we were there to make a demo tape. To lay three or four tracks down as quickly and cheaply as possible in order to use them as publicity and to get more gigs. There's a huge difference between the two. Mainly cost!

Anyway we got set up, and the tape began with Fang asking if this was the studio and that there wasn't enough room to swing a cat. Then it kicks off. We chose four tracks

"Space Invaders", a comedy poem of mine set to music that blatantly uses the theme from the movie "Close Encounters of the Third Kind."

"Groundhog Blues", a song written by Fang about buying a lump of dope only to discover that it was a lump of rubber from a Dunlop Groundhog car tyre (he always claimed this was a true story).

Then there was something called "Amazing Ilkley Rigs", which was an acapella number that started with us singing "Ilkley Moor Bah T'at" to the tune of "Amazing Grace" and then merging it into "London Town", a traditional folk song concerning a young man who goes to London and ends up being conned by a prostitute. Bellowhead did a good version a few years ago.

Finally we end with our version of Joni Mitchells "Big Yellow Taxi" performed as a sort of doo-wop song.

"Space Invaders" had become really popular at our gigs. I'd written it back in Harrogate as a protest poem about how space invader machines were turning pubs into amusement arcades. It was John who first suggested adding the theme music from "Close Encounters of the Third Kind" to it and it really worked. The rest of the band added the throbbing, repetitive beat with Fang adding the crashing noise by kicking his valve amp to get the effect. I sort of chanted the words in a strange quasi London accent. It worked even better live as we all moved sideways across the stage folding our arms and flapping them out to emulate the movement of a little space invader. It quickly caught on and as I performed it I would look out to the audience to see half of them copying us, just like rows of little space invaders. Even seated members of the audience would flap their arms.

I loved that number and always regret it never did get released as a single. I've never performed it since the demise of the Ferrets, mainly because it's not that brilliant without the music and effects, and let's face it, with the advent of computers and computer games does anyone actually remember space invaders? Mind you if the trend for retro gaming carries on I just might take it out and give it a trail run. For what it's worth here it is –

Space Invaders
There's UFO's in my local pub
There's aliens lurking in the snug
Space invaders in the public bar
These Jap machines they go too far
Zap... bang... pow... crash

I'll make those bloody spaceships crash
If only I can find the cash
Interstellar cosmic fun
I like to make those spaceships run
Zap... bang... pow... crash

Interstellar cosmic blitz
Space invaders gets on me tits
Noisy little green machines
Now I know what galactic means
Zap... bang... pow... crash

Micro chips and nuclear f.f.f.fission
Now you can get them on your television
The barman thinks that he's Darth Vader
And it's all because of space invaders
Zap... bang... pow... crash

I'm fed up with darts and being the chalker
Cos I wanna be like Luke Skywalker
And up in space behind protective screens
The aliens play at space machines

Zap... bang... pow... crash

Flying saucers and battleships too
They're all out to vaporise you
When you go off with a mighty bang
Remember the warning The Ferrets sang
Zap... bang... pow... crash... owwww.....
Graham Rhodes

We did a couple of gigs at private parties. One was on an island in the middle of the River Thames, it might have been Ham Island. The booking came from a friend of a friend of a fan. As it happened Dave Pruckner came down from Leeds for it. Everything was fine until we got to the actual riverbank and looked across to the Island. The same question was on everyone's lips. How the hell do we get across the river! Someone from the party had been despatched to meet us and they explained there was a rowing boast that would take us and the equipment across the water. Luckily enough that night the Thames was reasonably calm and not in flood. Getting across proved to be a bit like the old puzzle of the grain the chicken and the fox. Eventually the gear and the band were all at the other side. I went across sitting on a wooden seat holding onto an amp and hoping against hope that the boat would stop rocking and that neither myself nor the amp would end up in the water. The two things that caused most of the trouble were John and his Prophet Five and Fangs valve amp. I climbed out of the boat and willing hands helped with the amp, carrying it up a muddy path to a clearing in the middle of the island. It was surrounded by trees and bushes and lit by coloured lights. The performance was on a small stage area built at one end of the clearing. We gathered at the small bar that was built on one side of the area.

We played the gig and everything went fine. I can't remember who the audience were. I know they didn't sit and watch us, they sort of wandered around chatting, occasionally walking forward to our small stage and looking up at us more out of curiosity than in any interest in what we were doing. We were simply the background noise to a private party.

After it ended we all managed to get off the island without anyone falling into the river or dropping any gear. In fact the only thing out of the normal was that Dave and Mike appeared to get very drunk and mess around hiding in the bushes and jumping out at passers-by, which were mainly the other members of the band.

The second private party was for a cricket club do. Over at the Police management team, Nick Jones loved cricket and played for an occasional team that included musicians and management people called The Heavy Rollers. We turned up at some South London cricket ground and set up as the game was coming to a finish. The first thing I noticed was that the actual cricket game seemed to be a glorified excuse for a lot of drinking. No one seemed too sure of the score and people seemed to wander out into the field at random. Vermilion being one of them. For some reason she insisted that she should bowl and proceeded to almost take the head off the unfortunate bloke standing in front of her with only a cricket bat for defence. Anyway we set up and played where we were told to. Again we seemed to go down rather well. Various members of the cricket team came onto the stage and played with us including Vermilion and Nick who rattled off a drunken and raucous version of "Good Golly Miss Molly".

By now we were playing gigs all over London and even venturing into the deep South East, we played as far as Medway, Chatham, and Southend. By now we had managed to buy an old, beaten up, long wheel based, transit van. When I say beaten up I'm not exaggerating. At one point the floor on the passenger side fell out and we replaced it with flattened beer cans. As you can imagine it wasn't that solid and every time the van got up to sixty miles per hour it flapped, which wasn't bad when it was dry, but if it rained it let in a whole load of water. Sitting in the passenger seat was a hit and miss affair. It usually fell to me as I knew where the gig was and I could read maps, bear in mid this was well before the days of GPS and sat-nav.

It was around this time a fan stepped forward and offered to roadie for us. He took charge of the van and the driving, looked after the gear, and in his way, looked after us. Unfortunately I cannot remember his name. His real name that is. There is a reason for this. The very first gig he did with us was in central London. It was in Selfridge's staff canteen and was in honour of the Royal Wedding of Charles and Diana. To celebrate this upcoming Royal event the management of Selfridges decided to treat their staff. Every day during the week of the wedding they put a gig on in the staff restaurant. Two shows, one for 12.00 - 1.00pm and one for 1.00pm - 2.00pm. To please all tastes, each gig featured a different genre of music. There was a rock band, a classical group, a country group, and we were chosen to represent folk music!

After a harrowing drive through the West End of London we eventually got to Selfridges and were shown where to park and where we were performing and we began to set up. Then we realised we were missing a bit of vital equipment. Our new roadie had forgotten to pack the mixer. He was despatched back to the rehearsal space to pick it up (travelling via tube and taxi) and we did the best we could without it. He arrived back with it halfway through our first half set. It was then that someone, maybe Fang, maybe me, maybe someone else, decided to call him Kenwood. Get it? Kenwood Mixers! We all thought this was hilarious and the name stuck. From that day on as far as the band were concerned his name was Kenwood and his real name was forgotten. To us it was natural but it was hammered home just how much we had changed the guy when, some months later, at some outdoor festival, type gig we heard a voice over the tannoy saying -

"Will Mr Ken Wood, from Arkwright's Ferret please come to the organisers tent."

It never dawned on anyone in the band that people who weren't in on the joke would actually think his real name was Ken Wood. I often wonder whatever became of him and whether, once the madness of the Ferrets passed him by, he reverted back to his real name.

Kenwood also had a starring role in another gig we played when we were supported by a group of mummers. Now, just in case you have no idea of what mumming is; Mummers' plays are folk plays performed by troupes of amateur actors, traditionally all male, known as mummers or guisers. It refers particularly to a play in which a number of characters are called on stage, two of whom engage in a combat, the loser being revived by a doctor character. Originally they were popular in Europe and were bands of masked persons who during winter festivals paraded the streets and entered houses to dance or play dice.

Now this particular group claimed to be a traditional act and performed a typical mummers play featuring St George, a Turk, a Doctor and other interested parties. It was hilarious. Normally you'd come across this sort of thing outside in some market square, or on a village green, not in the back room of a pub on a stage two sizes too small for them. The first thing that went wrong was that whoever was in charge of their props had forgotten to bring the doctors bag. In desperation they looked around for some sort of substitute. The only thing they could find was our roadie's metal tool box that contained spare leads, gaffer tape, screwdrivers, an electric drill, and, in case of accidents, a first aid kit. Kenwood willingly lent it to them as we all sat in the audience watching on.

To say they were under rehearsed would be an exaggeration. There was a basic structure, but for the most part it seemed like highly decorative, experimental improvisation. The more they tried the stranger it got. It shambled along until it reached the point where St George died and they called for the Doctor to "cure" him. The doctor walked on and picked up his doctor's case (our metal tool box) that a member of their cast had inadvertently left sitting next to a large heater. Without looking he bent down, picked it up, gave a sort of strangled scream, half of pain, half of shock and threw the metal box in an arc off the stage into the audience. Luckily enough the audience saw it coming and scattered. It crashed to the ground where we could see the metal handle glowing with the heat from the heater. The audience were then treated to seeing five minutes of Kenwood applying some sort of cream and bandages to the doctor's badly burned hand. They continued, but by then they had lost both momentum and audience interest. They were so woefully inept we booked them to support us at another gig.

This time they were even funnier. When it was their turn to perform they appeared at the back of the audience with six of them holding up poles on which was balanced a horse's skin. A real horse's skin! As soon as they entered the room the audience began sniffing the air and glancing at each other. It smelt bloody awful. Then, as they moved toward the stage, a member of the audience, whether by accident or design, stepped onto the horses tail. The skin slid to the floor behind them whilst the six blokes continued moving towards the stage still holding the six poles aloft.

The smell of the skin was so awful that the club organisers stepped in and demanded they take it out of the room immediately. When they explained that they couldn't do their play without the horses skin the organisers told them that they were prepared to forego that pleasure, and that they could go away and take the skin with them. The club had to take a break to deploy air fresheners before the show could go on. I asked one of the troupe where they got the horse's skin from. He told me they bought it from a slaughter house. I asked them if they didn't think to get it cured. They said they had. It had been nailed to the roof of a shed for the last two months!

Around that period of the Ferrets I was aware that I was drinking quiet heavily before I went on stage. I was almost at that stage of believing I wasn't funny until I was semi drunk. This was due to the pressure of performing, but also, strangely enough due to me being a Yorkshireman. Let me explain. Every folk club we played was in a pub that boasted at least one "real ale". Now this phrase was new to me. Bear in mind in the late seventies and early eighties there were no micro breweries. "Real Ale" was still a novelty. It was the age of Watney's, Courage and other big breweries. Of course in London there was Fullers, and Young's, occasionally there was Shepherd Neame and Adnams. For reasons still beyond me as soon as I opened my mouth and approached the bar the organiser would single me out always saying the same thing –

"Oh, you're from Yorkshire, you must have a pint of....."

and then direct me towards a pint of dubious something or other. Something strong that I'd neither heard of nor wanted. But a free pint is a free pint. It resulted in me drinking all sorts of different beers of different strengths and different tastes. To avoid the madness of this beer roulette I began drinking Barley Wine. You don't see it these days, but it used to be sold in small bottles or cans, and it was bloody strong. I was now at the point where it took two cans to get me on the stage, before performing. I knew I needed to cut back. Mikes drinking was also getting heavier and was becoming a problem. We noticed that on some numbers he was forgetting the words. Sometime he missed rehearsals. We had to have a word with him, give him a warning and lay down some rules.

As our fame spread Arkwright's Ferret was becoming the Marmite of the South Eastern folk scene. People either loved us or hated us. The traditionalists hated us. We mixed rock with folk, we mixed in comedy and poetry, we did cheap visual gags and didn't take the genre seriously enough. Even in 1981, folk music was divided between traditional and contemporary styles despite the advent and acceptance of bands like Fairport Convention, Steeleye Span, Gryphon, Mr Fox, and Dr Cosgill. Indeed some folk clubs didn't allow electric bands to play, and over at Cecil Sharpe House, Ewan MacColl didn't allow electric instruments within a mile of the place, despite the fact that members of the aforesaid bands were sitting upstairs in the library researching old tunes and songs that they could electrify.

There's an interesting insight into this element when I look at the reviews we were receiving and the letters we got after our gigs.

"The Ferret are gaining in stature with every gig & with the death of Dr Cosgill about to be announced in September (The cure of not enough work around the clubs couldn't be found) the Ferrets should take their place with a vengeance.... Catch them around the Kent area soon. I was surprised when "traditionalist" Ernie Warner booked 'em immediately after seeing them at

Gillingham. But they are folk and his audience will love them"
Extract from a review in July/August Kasebook written by Sue Duff.

"The Ferret provided an evening of songs, poems, humour and electrics at our club. They were enjoyed by all but the most diehard of traddies (after all, you're not here to enjoy yourself, this is a folk club), & although I was fondled on the buttocks several times, I shall be having them back.
Nigel Chippendale organiser Charlwood Folk Club (Rising Sun)

Just two of the letters that show the divide between traditional and contemporary folk was still alive and well in 1982.

Despite our earlier warnings Mikes drinking was becoming more and more of a problem. He continued turning up late for gigs, missing rehearsals and missing his cues on stage. His performances and behaviour were becoming more and more erratic. Eventually, and with great sadness tinged with annoyance we came to a mutual agreement, and Mike left the band. It presented a problem for us as not only had we lost his material, we had also lost the vocal harmony that balanced out between Fang and Chris. Due to the amount of gigs we had in advanced bookings we needed someone and needed them fast.

The solution was right in front of our eyes. My wife Jane, (We'd married back in 1981). She had heard more Arkwright's Ferret than anyone else, more than anyone who wasn't in the band should have. It was logical, she knew the material and she could sing, oh and she wanted to. It was a no brainer. After a couple of rehearsals she fitted in perfectly. We reworked some of the older material like "Bonny Light horseman!", and added new traditional material such as the song "Hawkstowe Grange", from where

Steeleye Span took their name, and a song called "The Painful Plough".

Another traditional song that received an updated Ferret treatment was called "Farewell Parker" (although that might have been the title we gave it. I have found the original lyrics under the heading of "Admiral Duncan"). We had done a version of this earlier but now we really rocked it, but the thing that gave this song its unique place in our repertoire were the actions we gave to the words of the chorus.

The chorus went -

"Farewell Parker, thou bright angel
once thou was old England's pride
although he was hanged up for mutiny
worse than him
was left behind."

The actions were as follows -
　　Farewell (we waved at the audience)
　　Thou (point at the audience)
　　Bright (shield our eyes,)
　　Angel (wave out hands like wings)
　　Once (Finger up to denote one)
　　Thou (point at audience again)
　　Was Old England's (Bend over and pretend to use a walking stick)
　　Pride (stick chest out and salute)
　　Although he was hanged up (Pretend to be hanging by holding hand over head and tilting head to one side)
　　For mutiny (Fang and I would pretend to knee each other in the balls)

Worse than him (members of the band would point at each other)
Was left behind (all band members would bend over and point at their left buttock!)

Yes it was corny, but the audiences loved it, especially when we would begin the song by taking them step by step, through the actions and getting them to join in. Many a pint would be spilt as the band encouraged the audience to point at their own left buttocks. I think we had as much fun with this as they did.

We also re-introduced our cover version of the Roy Harper song "When an Old Cricketer Leaves the Crease" into the set as the high notes were now covered.

Despite the loss of Mike none of our regular "fans" seemed to mind and the new Arkwright's Ferret went back on the road stronger and better. The band gigged long and hard up and down the South of England and throughout London. Now we were playing clubs for the second or third time, and over the years many of these gigs seemed to merge into one. I know we played Croydon Folk Club more than once because, although I remember nothing about the club I do remember that we managed to lock ourselves out of our van and had to enlist the help of a very kind and patient policeman who eventually showed us how to break into our own van with the help of a wire coat hanger.

For some reason we were very popular in Harlow. We played the Square One Club there a number of times, and we did a charity busk on a Saturday in the middle of Harlow New Town. One time while playing at the Square One Club we were recorded and broadcast live by a local hospital radio station. As we could see the hospital from the venue we included them in the show and asked the patients and listeners to switch their lights on and off so we could see them. Never for a minute did we expect anyone would actually do it. But they did, quite a few of them.

By now looking after the Ferrets had become a full time job and I had ended my employment at the audio visual company to look after them. I did keep on my freelance commitments though and still continued working for Miles Copeland and his record label, but I was beginning to feel the strain. Trying to keep the momentum of performing and getting gigs to meet the expectations of the band was a difficult juggling act.

Interest in us began to grow and we were contacted by the folk reporter of the Melody maker, they wanted Fang and myself to drop into their office to do an interview. Wow, a full page interview in the Melody Maker. We both felt like real rock stars as we presented ourselves at reception and were shown through the office to meet Patrick Humphries who back then was the folk reporter, now he's a noted rock journalist with many books behind him. It was during this interview that he labelled us as "New Traditionalists." It was a great article and did us a lot of good. Bookings and interest in us grew.

Another iconic place we played was The Half Moon at Putney. Since I first arrived in London I'd been a fan of that venue. It was legendary. On many Monday nights well before the band existed I'd been there to watch the wonderful Bob Kerr's Whoopee Band. It was made up of past members of The New Vaudeville Band (of "Winchester Cathedral" fame), The Temperance Seven (of "Pasadena" and "Finchley Central" fame) and The Bonzo Dog Doo Dah Band. How could anyone not like them? Not only were they great players of 20's style comedy jazz, they also used sight gags, props, and general lunacy to such a great effect that you began laughing the moment they started to ten minutes after they'd finished.

The Half Moon was, in many ways, the unofficial top folk venue of London and Arkwright's Ferret had to play quite a few support spots there before we got to headline. As an important venue the place was the drinking home to many folk artists who lived at that end of London and the place used to stage "special" gigs. Some artists would use the venue to test out new material or as a warm up gig before they set out on a tour. These gigs were never advertised. Instead news spread by word of mouth. We were tipped off about one such gig that was to be held the night before we did our first headliner there. I'm not sure which members of the band went. I can only remember sitting next to Fang as we had managed to wangle front row seats. As we settled down the secret gig began and onto the stage walked John Martyn, behind him playing double bass was Danny Thompson, and on drums, sitting only a few feet away from us was Phil Collins. It was the debut gig of the tour that was promoting John Martyn's new album, "Grace and Danger".

The trio played the entire album and between numbers John Martyn did his usual thing of chatting to the audience whilst rolling up a joint. He'd then light it, take a couple of toke's before sticking the joint onto the end of one of his guitar strings up by the machine heads. Fang and I looked at each other and nodded. Sure enough on his seventh number John Martyn went to stick his joint on a guitar string that wasn't there, looked at the six joints already dancing around, shrugged, looked down on the audience and passed it to Fang, who took a couple of tokes and passed it to me and then I passed it on.

The following night it was the turn of Arkwright's Ferret to top the bill at the Half Moon Putney. For us it was a big deal and we were all nervous. As we walked onto the stage Fang tripped over a lead, stumbled, and almost fell over. There was a gasp from the audience. Then, as he stood up, he came out with one of the best ad libs that ever emerged from his lips.

"I didn't fall, I was here for John Martyn last night and I was looking for the dope he dropped!"

The audience laughed. We'd broken the ice and the gig went brilliantly, with one slight exception, when we sang the words of "Blue Suede Shoes" to the tune of Ralph McTell's song "From Clare to Here." Ralph McTell himself rose up out of the audience and walked out.

"Sod him if he can't take a joke!" was the bands reaction.

We extended our range of gigs. One time we drove all the way to Poole in Dorset. The only thing I remember about that journey was that we passed Stonehenge and feeling very unimpressed with it. It seemed so small from the road.

We played as far West as Bournemouth. We played somewhere on the South Coast called Portland that turned out to be a tied island four miles long, five miles south of Weymouth and attached to the rest of the United Kingdom by a road along a long strip of shingle called Chesil Beach. It's famous but we never got a chance to look around. Our bass player Doug, who was travelling separately with his girl friend Steph, broke down on his journey. Of course, as these were pre-mobile phone days, we didn't know that until we arrived at the venue, a small pub up a damn great hill. We knew it was a damn great hill because halfway up it our van gave a cough and promptly died. I walked up to the venue and explained our predicament. The organisers and half the audience followed me out of the pub and down the hill where they all worked together and pushed the van to the doors of the pub. As we unloaded we got the message about Doug. It seemed as if the gig was doomed. However never underestimate the improvisation power of the Ferret. Fang and I had words and we agreed that we would sing the bass line introductions to the songs which John would pick up on the keyboards. We did it and it worked and the audience loved it. Once again we had pulled it off. Doug eventually arrived and plugged in for the second half of the show and I'm sure some of the audience were disappointed.

We played the Hastings Poetry and Folk festival (as it seemed it was especially created for a band like us!). When we arrived we found ourselves in some sort of formal gathering where the Festival organiser, various dignitaries and the Lord Mayor were waiting to greet us. For reasons best known to himself, for the entirety of this civic reception Fang insisted on wearing roller skates and boxing gloves. Somewhere in the annals of the local Hastings press there is a photograph of the Lord Mayor looking bemused as he tried to shake hands with this large hairy individual wearing boxing gloves whilst the rest of us stood around them grinning. The gig was fine with the exception of a woman at the back who seemed to feint and fell forward hitting her face on the back of the seat in front of her. It was strange as I was looking at her as she did it. It seemed like slow motion and before I could shout out she'd fallen. I think she broke her nose as I could hear the crack of her face hitting the back of the seat from the stage. We had to stop for a while, I think we took an early break, as the paramedics took her away to hospital.

As I mentioned previously some folk clubs didn't like electric bands. We arrived at one somewhere south of London and were dragging the equipment through the bar to the room where the folk club was when the organiser came running up.

"Don't let the landlord see the equipment."

We looked at each other. By now with the luxury of a van, the equipment had grown to John's Prophet 5 plus amp. Fangs acoustic guitar, and a Vox valve amp, the mixing desk, Doug's Bass guitar and amp, a mandolin, Chris's electric guitar and amp, plus a PA, various leads, mics and mic stands, all of which was sat in the middle of the pub floor. Before we could say anything the landlord appeared and descended on the folk club organiser.

"They're electric!" he wailed. *I've told you, no electric bands!"*

I watched on as the folk club organiser seemed to wilt. I didn't need to be psychic to predict that the next thing to happen was for us to get sent back home without getting paid. I had to do something. I stepped forward.

"What is it about electric bands?" I asked, expecting to get drawn into the argument of traditional versus contemporary folk once again.

He turned towards me *"You'll use my electricity. I have to pay the bill!"* he declared.

Quick as a flash I answered back *"But we only use one plug!"*

He thought about it for a few seconds whilst I tried to keep a straight face. I daren't look at any other members of the band. I daren't even look at the folk club organiser. The landlord suddenly nodded his head.

"One plug you say? Oh well, that's alright then!" He replied and disappeared off leaving us to sct up.

Which we did! True to my word, we ran the entire rig from just one plug and a network of extension leads. That night, as we played the set, from the stage you could tell where the ring main was located. It was where the wall was so warm members of the audience were moving away from it. It's a wonder we never blew the place up, or at least blew a couple of fuses, but no, our luck held. We played, we went down very well, and we got paid.

We had another strange request at the Greenwich Folk Club that was held in an upstairs room in an old pub a couple of streets away from where the Cutty Sark is permanently moored. We were halfway through our first set when the landlord appeared on the scene to ask us if we could stop jumping around, otherwise he'd have to stop the gig. When we asked why it turned out that directly below us was a dining room that was lit by an antique chandelier. Our movement, combined with the vibrations of the music, was making the thing swing around in a manner that alarmed the landlord so much he was scared that it would crash to the floor in the same manner as that famous "Only Fools and Horses" sketch. We had a quick chat between us on stage. To save the gig we decided that we wouldn't move and to play the rest of the gig as if we were all Gene Vincent impersonators. One leg thrust forward and one behind. It was just possible that we looked cool, however I have a feeling that we probably looked like a bunch of idiots. At least we completed the gig and got paid.

Just down the street from us in Dukes Avenue lived another musician who had some interesting contacts. He was called Mickey Keen and laid claim that he had been a member of the 60's band The Ivy League and more recently of Hudson Ford. He first discovered Arkwright's Ferret when we played a street party in our own street, for the Charles and Di Royal Wedding. He was interested in what we did and always kept in touch and up to date with what we were doing. He had his own connections and complications in his life. One of his close friends was Elaine Page who, back then seemed to lean heavily on him, much to the annoyance of Mickey's wife. The two of them had met when they were both involved in a production of "Hair". For reasons best known to himself Mickey had built himself a rifle range at the bottom of his garden claiming it helped reduce tension. I tried it a few times and, oddly enough, it did, although the person in the house behind him was often knocking on his door complaining about lead pellets. I found a better way of calming myself through the help of Mickey's wife who used to teach meditation techniques based on some sort of Sufi philosophy. Anyhow Mickey knew someone who had a recording studio and he managed to arrange some cheap recording time for us in down time, that magical time between 6.00pm and 6.00am. It was explained that we could only use eight tracks, so we decided the best thing to do was record the strongest numbers in our set, the ones we knew inside out and record them more or less live, but allow time for over dubs on the vocals. That would be our first album. We planned it very carefully before we went anywhere near to the studio, so when we arrived we were prepared and could get right down to the recording. I learnt a valuable lesson from Mickey in that session. As we began he placed a large round clock on the mixing desk.

"Every time that minute hand moves you've spent money!" he announced.

By God that focused us. In my later career whenever I found myself in a recording studio I remembered Mickey and that clock. We piled into the studio at 6.00pm and by seven had set up and by eight got the levels right and were ready to roll. It must have been on the second or third number that we ran into a problem. It was on a track called "Rambling Sailor", somehow we discovered that

John should be playing mandolin and keyboards at the same time. We scratched our heads. When we played it live he just dropped the keyboards and, after the mandolin break, went back to them, but for some reason in the studio it didn't sound right. Of course that's always the way in a studio, you get creative and that's when the problems begin and the costs start to rise. I'd already experienced this when I was recording my poem "Mirror Man". For some reason Mickey thought it needed echo and a second vocal track to create effects. I didn't think it needed it, but he was producing us and the "as we're in a studio lets use it" attitude prevailed. It's there. I still don't think it needed it. Hey ho!

It was whilst we were pondering John's problem when a man who was in the studio stepped forward and offered to help. He'd finished his own session in the studio next door and had been standing at the back of the control room listening to what we were doing. He offered to play the keyboards for us. John explained what was needed and, after a quick run through, he filled in. The session went fine and we nailed it and moved onto the next track. The guy asked if he could stay and contributed to a number of the tracks. Eventually he had to leave and we carried on recording and then mixing down the tracks.

Later as we played the tracks back somebody mentioned the guy and asked who he was.

"Oh him, he's always doing stuff around here, his name's Billy Ocean!" Came the reply.

Bloody Hell! Billy Ocean played on our recordings!

Once the recordings were mixed, and whilst we were waiting for various people in various record companies to listen to them, we ran off a large number of cassette copies, planning on selling them at our upcoming gigs. Merchandise!

We had also produced a little leaflet that we called "The Arkwright's Ferret Official Souvenir Programme", that contained some of my poems and some of Fangs lyrics illustrated by myself and Chris. There were also photographs and little joke biographies of band members and a potted history of the band. The centre spread was a photograph of the band playing in the performance space of the 17th century St Pauls Church, facing the old Covent Garden market buildings full of tourist shops and people looking down on the piazza from the balcony of the Punch and Judy Pub. It was a novelty as, back then, the Covent Garden we know today had only been opened for two years. We'd been invited to play there as a part of London's Folk Week when a number of folk acts played a full set where so many buskers have, and still are performing. Personally it was an amazing experience for me, to stand and recite my poetry on such an historic spot and look up at the people on the balcony and standing around us. It was probably the largest crowd we'd ever played to.

As it came around to our second year as a full band we planned the second Arkwright's Ferret Birthday Bash and decided to hold it in a venue we had played a few times, an Arts Centre in Archway. It was here in our early days that we had met a bloke who wanted to drum for us. Every time we played there he tried to persuade us that we needed a drummer, and he was available. We didn't. We had nothing against drummers, however many of the clubs we played were small and as it was we were a six piece band with gear that took up space, if we took on board a drummer we would lose those gigs as we simply wouldn't fit in. Also a drummer and his kit would take up vital room in the van, and take time setting up and breaking down the kit. Finally, and probably the more important thing of all, was that we all thought the sound of Arkwright's Ferret was full enough without the addition of drums. Drums would alter our sound and we were happy with how we sounded. No, the last thing we needed was a drummer. It turned out that the drummer was, in his way, famous. He used to be the drummer with the Pretty Things, a sixties R & B band who I thought, and still think, were one of the best bands of that period. Certainly rivals to the Rolling Stones, who ironically enough, some members had played with as they settled their respective line-ups in their very early days. The guy used to wear a little badge that read "Yes I am Viv Prince, No I'm not dead... yet!"

The actual birthday gig was held on Saturday 13th Feb 1982. The bill was excellent.

The James Smith Experience, billed as contemporary songs, breaks the barrier of folk with hilarity.

Catcherman – a hard driven R& B duo that used an early computer to provide their driving beats.

Peter Buckley-Hill a comedy singer songwriter that had supported the Ferrets a number of times.

Deidre Simpson a part of the growing alternative cabaret circuit, comedienne, singer, dancer, mime artist. She always finished her act by playing a ukulele whilst standing on her head.

Then, top of the bill - Arkwright's Ferret.

The whole thing was introduced by an act called Ken the Clown with Toby the Wonder Dog. All this for just £2.00 with a 20p discount for members! This time we filled the place, the gig was a huge success.

We were riding high, although, as I've already said I was under pressure and that pressure was having a detrimental effect on my marriage. I'd already experienced one tail spin. I'd been drinking in the Windsor Castle with a young man who was on his way the fight in the Falklands and I got drunk with him. Then I went across to the rehearsal rooms and something cracked. I flung a tin of white paint across the room. It hit a far wall and the paint splashed down. No equipment was damaged, not even splashed, however Jane decided this was evidence of my impending madness. For some reason, and without my agreement, I found myself being despatched to friends back in Harrogate. I spent a few days drinking with Stuart and playing pool with Neil Simone. I caused a panic for the two friends when, after a visit to my old art college I told them I'd been offered a teaching job. They politely informed me I couldn't stay any longer and that evening I caught the train back to London. In actual fact I had planned on going back anyway but I wanted to test their tolerance of me. I had and found it wanting. I'm not too sure I ever met up with them again.

When I got back to London the band had some gigs to do and it was on the way back home from one of them that John and Doug told me that Chris and Jane had been having an affair. For some time they had travelled separately from the rest of the band, Jane's excuse was that they both had work on the following morning and, as they didn't have to wait for the gear to be loaded it was quicker. They usually got home at least an hour before us. Like an idiot I suspected nothing. Of course I was the last to know. I was shattered. I knew things were bad but I hadn't expected to be betrayed by both my wife and the bloke that I trusted and accepted as both a friend and a workmate. Especially as I had invited him to London, given him a place to live, sorted him out a job, and given him a place in the band. I felt like the rug had been pulled out from under my world. Doug and John were surprised at my reaction. For some reason they had assumed that I knew about it. When they realised I didn't and that they too had been fooled by a false assumption, they weren't happy. When we reached Dukes Avenue John, accompanied by Kenwood, rushed upstairs and immediately sacked the pair of them from the band. I did nothing I was too stunned by the revelations and too upset to take a part in the discussions. Fang said nothing but sat on the fence. I left it to the rest of the band to sort out the future.

Despite my own personal anguish there were some commitments that needed fulfilling. Most notably there were some dates in the Midlands at clubs we'd never played before. We needed replacements. Fang had an idea. He suggested that we should go down the Tube and find a couple of suitable players who were busking. We did, and within a day found what we were looking for, a guitarist and a fiddle player. We quickly organised a couple of rehearsals and off we went. There was just one problem. At the rehearsal the fiddle player used an acoustic fiddle, on the actual gig he played and electric fiddle. Suddenly we were a different band. I remember turning to Fang during the first number and asking when had we become the Pink Floyd? We completed the gigs and returned to London. Jane had now moved upstairs in the house to be with Chris leaving me to live downstairs. It was too painful for me and I spent many nights down the street at Mickey's place where his wife tried to keep my brains in my head with frequent Sufi meditations. A ferret fan thinking of my situation brought me a cat. It moved in with me.

Then Fang had a bleak moment and made a half hearted suicide attempt. We all knew it was a cry for help and for attention. There was nothing I could do about it. I was too far gone in my own problems. I left him to Chris and Jane to cope with. After all it was their actions that had helped to destroy the band, and, in their own way, damaged Fang's delicate mental stability. I'd had enough and had decisions to make to protect my own sanity. I hung around in Finchley just as long as it took for me to find accommodation in a squat in Streatham, south of the river and the other side of London. I took the cat up north to my parents and left it there. It had a long, happy and very spoilt life. For the rest of its days, every time I visited, it hid until it was sure I wasn't going to take it back to London.

Once in Streatham I made a couple of telephone calls. Within the week I picked up a freelance job in an audio-visual company in Seven Dials working on the product launch of the new Ford Sierra. I was now back working in the audio-visual, conference staging industry and that left no time for bands or poetry or regrets. It was so full on that I even had to end my freelance relationship with Miles Copeland, Nick and Vermillion and The Police.

For the next few years I became an audio-visual designer, working for some of London's top conference production companies. It was hard work, it was creative, exhilarating and well paid. I was sent all over Europe and the UK directing photo shoots. When not travelling I was at my drawing board hard at designing art-work and images. I worked with some brilliant photographers, board artists and fellow designers and did some amazing things and saw some amazing places. I worked for a variety of clients that anyone would give their right arm for, clients such as Ford, Volvo, Rolls Royce, British Airways, British Aerospace, Coca Cola, and its rival Pepsi, British Rail and British Rail Property Board. My CV grew at an alarming rate. Not only did I become a audio-visual producer, director and designer but I also became a scriptwriter. I stopped grieving about the ex-wife and Arkwright's Ferret and for the next ten years or so I never wrote a word of poetry.

I became a scriptwriter more by accident than design. It was a case of me and my big mouth. As a freelance audio-visual designer I was given the job of designing a conference for British Airways, it was the launch of a new route into America from Gatewick. I was told by the marketing department that the concept was "Route 66". Brilliant! I got a Rolling Stones sound alike band into a studio to record the song "Route 66" and sent an American photographer the length of Route 66 to take the shots. Unfortunately there wasn't enough money in the budget for me to go along and direct him. Anyway I created a visual treat cutting the images to the music. It looked great. With three days to go, before the show went off to the location of the conference, I came back from lunch to find the directors looking at the show slides in position on my light box. They were not looking happy. When I asked what was wrong I was told that the new British Airways route didn't go anywhere near Route 66, it didn't even fly over it. Then they asked me to change the concept.

I went bloody ballistic. It was impossible! They were looking at three months work, that couldn't be redone inside three days. Unrepentant they told me to come up with something and I stomped off to the pub. After three bottle of Grolsh I had an idea. If the bosses of British Airways didn't realise the new air route didn't go near Route 66 then it was plausible that no one else would. I got hold of the band and got them back into the studio where I wrote an extra verse to the song Route 66 putting into the verse this particular towns name. Then I got the slide show to be reprogrammed, just adding a few slides. It worked. I called the senior management in to look at the result. They agreed, as they heard the town's name in the song no one questioned it.

The show ran in front of five hundred travel agents and the senior staff of British Airways, no one did notice. I'd got away with it. After at the debrief I threw one of the biggest artistic wobblers I'd ever thrown in my life. Towards the end I heard my own voice say the words *"from now on I'll write my own scripts!"*

I stopped as the words I'd just spoken sank in. Even worse the senior management agreed. I got sent on a brief scriptwriting course with the in-house script writer. From that day on I was a scriptwriter. It did have its up-side. For a start it increased my earnings, and I got to go on lots of research recce's. It also led to an attempt to reunite myself and Fang. David Sandison, the man who taught me scriptwriting had a few fingers in a few pies. In addition to writing the book on the artist David Oxtoby, at one stage of his life he had been the PR man for the Rolling Stones and then Lynyrd Skynyrd, and currently was managing a couple of American acts, Wes McGee being one of them. Anyway he knew of the Ferrets and had an idea for a novelty Christmas single. We got in touch with Fang and we wrote and recorded a parody of Steeleye Span's Christmas hit "Gaudette." We recorded it with some musicians and a girl singer, but, despite it being touted to many record companies, it never got released. That recording session was the last time I ever saw Fang.

So what happened to the rest of the band? Well, Fang became a professional busker in and around the Archway area of London. He died in 2014.

John returned to the computer industry, married and raised kids. He's now happily retired.

Jane returned to social work and Chris stayed at the audio-visual company in Goldhawk Road. Sometime in the late eighties or nineties they left London and opened a model car museum somewhere in the Midlands. Jane died in the early 2012.

I've no idea what happened to Doug, or Kenwood.

Mike Hurrey took his own life in the early 1980's.

Did Arkwright's Ferret change the world? Did it alter the perception of folk music? The answer is no, of course not. Did it leave a legacy, again I have the feeling the answer is no. Perhaps if we'd gone on for another couple of years, maybe. I do know that we created a fan base, and played to a lot of people who enjoyed what we did, and perhaps, in the long run that's all one can ask.

As an interesting footnote years later I was on a train when Martin Carthy, the father and godfather of English folk music, got on and sat opposite me. I nodded at him, aware I was in the presence of folk royalty. He said hello and looked at me.

"I think I know you!" He said

I shook my head. *"I very much doubt it"*. I replied, *"but I know you!"*

As the train pulled out of York station he looked at me once again and shook his head. *"I'm sure I know you!"*

I looked at him. *"Well I was on the folk circuit once. I was in a band called Arkwright's Ferret!"*

He sat back in his seat and a distant looked crossed his face then he smiled. *"Bloody hell! Arkwright's Ferret! Whatever happened to them!"*

I think if you'd have told me back in the Orange Tree Folk Club that, in years to come, my band would be remembered by Martin Carthy, I would have settled for that.

Chapter 4
York 1987-2001

The next few years flashed by in a flurry of conference designs, product launches and audio-visual presentations. I directed art workers, photographers and programmers. I created animated art and business presentations. I became a script writer. I also met Sue and had a child with her. My daughter was born on May 8th 1984. We called her Samantha after my Grandfather Sam Gooch. Then, in the late 1980's, I was head hunted and found myself moving to York to head up a video and conference production company. I left London with mixed feelings. I felt I still hadn't done enough, and was going to miss some good friends. However the money offered wasn't to be sniffed at, and it was moving back up North. At least I would see my parents more than a couple of times a year.

Once again the demands on my creativity to both pitch for and win the business, write the scripts, direct and produce the conferences or videos left neither time nor inclination to write any poetry. Then two things happened. One good, one bad. I was contacted to produce a permanent installation audio-visual display for the reopening of London's Science Museum. The York firm were hesitant to let me go but the powers that be behind the project offered them the opportunity to make some equipment sales and, as I was soon to find out, they would rather sell equipment than deal with creative processes. So I got the job.

At the same time I came down with an illness called Immune

Throbocycopedic Pupura. I.T.P. for short. It was something to do with platelet's and red corpuscles At first the doctors at York hospital thought I had Leukaemia, and diagnosed me as such. Then after I'd taken that on board they changed their minds. It was I.T.P., but it was treatable, just. I was put on a huge dosage of steroids. One of the strongest dosages they'd ever given anyone in North Yorkshire. Every week I had to report to the doctors where my hair and nail growth were measured and recorded. The steroids seemed to kick my platelets into action but the bad news was it took a month or two to cure, and two years to come down from, by reducing the dosage bit by bit. In those two years I became two separate gorillas. I was sleeping two to three hours a day and eating five meals a day. I was making phone calls then, ten minutes later, making them again. The people I worked with put up with it, but as the Science Museum project was only three months long they didn't experience the worse of it. I was allowed to go down to London to supervise the installation of the equipment and to see my program run and to do the necessary fine tuning. It was a ten screen show run by thirty six projectors and took a hell of a lot of fine tuning. Then there was the opening. As designer I was asked to attend and then I received an official invite that required me to be presented to H.R.M. The Queen. That was a bit of a surprise!

The management of the York company, especially the directors and chairman were green with envy. At every meeting they kept telling me how proud my parents must be. They did however manage to wangle themselves an invite to the opening so they did see me shake the royal hand and do the royal head nod. As we shook hands she actually spoke to me. The Director of the Science Museum had introduced me as the designer of the audio-visual show she had started.

"Very Nice!" she said and moved on.

However evidently she meant it as, when it started, she put her glasses on, which I was informed later, meant she really wanted to see it.

The worst was the Duke of Edinburgh. For a start I was surprised at how tall he was. Then he asked the question I dreaded.

"How did you do it?"

How the hell do you explain a three month production process in less than a minute. I think I burbled something about it being a team effort and then he passed on, probably thinking I was some sort of idiot.

In addition to standing in line and having my hand shaken I was also directing a video of the opening event, so I met the Queen wearing a new suite and a small headphone set. Two things struck me about her. The first was that she was much smaller than I imagined. The second was that she was wearing old, worn shoes. For some bizarre reason I imagined she always wore new shoes!

Working whilst under the effect of steroids is not a good idea, I'm rather surprised I passed the Royal vetting system, but I did. However eating five meals a day and being completely out of control destroyed my relationship. Christ alone knows why doctors don't explain what's happening to someone when they prescribe such stuff, even better why don't they tell a partner what to expect?

I eventually left the York production company, due the fact the board, who had a mindset like a bunch of Victorian shopkeepers, realised that they didn't like creative people around and preferred selling equipment. I started freelancing as a scriptwriter and producer/director for a couple of Leeds production companies. In addition to creating a lot of corporate work I also worked on a couple of television documentaries.

I was living in Tockwith, a small village situated between York and Wetherby when poetry popped up into my life again. I was a regular in one of the two village pubs and probably through chatting to someone, I was asked to do a couple of poems at the annual Tockwith village show, between a couple of local bands. I agreed. The stage was the back of an open lorry which was fun, and my act seemed to go down OK. I kept it clean and did the Jonathon Cooper monologue and one other. Then I was asked to do a poetry reading in one of the pubs for Burns Night. I protested that I wasn't Scottish, but it was pointed out that I was a poet and that was the next best thing. I did Burns "Ode to a Haggis" and then some of my own stuff. I upset one of the rich locals by asking him to sit down adding we'd all seen his Christmas pullover. The rest of the pub laughed. He didn't speak to me again. Suddenly the bug of performing began to gnaw at me again. Living in Tockwith was a pain as York was the nearest large city. There was one bus every thirty minutes but the buses ended at 9.00pm and a cab ride back was £10.00 but York was where I needed to be, it was where the bands and the gigs were.

It was whilst I was living in Tockwith that I created my first books. They weren't literary masterpieces, in fact they weren't literary at all, they were photographic books. The first was published in 1993 and was called "Leeds Visible History - Industry, Enterprise & Endeavour." and comprised a series of photographs of Leeds that showed its history in chronological order. The first pictures being the site of the ancient battle of Winwead that occurred in AD 655 in the area of Leeds called Stanks, right outside the house I was born in, and went on through the years until it ended with a photograph of the latest city centre buildings. I managed to hustle myself a book launch and window display in the Leeds branch of Waterstone's that was attended by the Lady Mayor who gave my parents a little badge of a Leeds owl. That was one time they were very proud of me.

I did the second book a year later. It was the same format only this time it was "The Visual History of York – Walls and Windows Bars and Bridges." Again I had a book launch and window display, this time at the York Waterstone's. Copies of the two books are still around. Looking on Amazon I see that various second hand copies of the Leeds book can be bought from 90p to £14.99 whilst copies of the York book are available from £1.22 to £11.65.

The internet is an amazing thing. The same Google search reveals there are copies of both of my books in the National Library of Australia. Honest! How the hell they got there God only knows! I didn't believe it myself but here's a link to their archives just to prove it! https://trove.nla.gov.au/version/29134967

Despite the lack of public transport I began hanging around in Fibbers, one of the more famous York rock venues, during Saturdays, when it was open for coffee. It was a great venue for putting on new, upcoming bands and bands that were on their way back down. I've spent many a happy hour there watching gigs from a wide variety of my personal favourites, from Roy Harper to Kinky Friedman. Somehow I got myself booked to announce the bands and performers playing at an all day charity gig there and was able to slip a few poems into the proceedings. As I left the stage and walked towards the bar I was hailed by one of two guys sat at a table. I got my drink and joined them. They introduced themselves. One was called Dave Alderson who led a band called Aldo's Orphans. They specialised in cover versions of heavy rock songs by bands like Thin Lizzy and Whitesnake. The second was a guy called Gary Barrett, singer with his own band called Life

Support (or it might have been Stone Cold Sober, over the years Gary had a number of different lines ups in a number of different bands. He even had a Free tribute act called Free Spirit and a Beatles covers band called Pepperland). Anyway the pair of them liked my material and invited me to support their own bands, during their respective beer breaks. They both played regular gigs at a number of York pubs, but mainly The Roman Baths in St Sampson's Square, the pub with the remains of a genuine Roman Bath in the basement.

For the next five or six years I would have great fun supporting these two characters and their bands at many gigs, especially with Gary's various bands. He had a residency every Thursday night at The Roman Baths and a great following of fans that each week would pack the place out. I'd then get up in their beer break and do five or six poems. Sometimes I was heckled, but mostly they took to me, eventually I became a regular feature. There were other York venues I played, sometimes with them, sometimes without them. There were gigs at The Northern Wall, The White Swan, and The De Grey Rooms, The Red Horse up by Walmgate, which is now a Chinese restaurant. At the same venues I also supported a band called Hard Lines, a three piece band that did the best version of the song "Caledonia" I've ever heard.

Of course now I was back to performing poetry I needed to write new material. I've always responded to pressure by being able to write to order, to write to demand. Don't forget now I was a full time script writer used to working to tight deadlines. When you've a deadline you simply can't say you're not in the mood to write, or that you're waiting for a mythical muse. Try that one and you simply won't work again! Being a scriptwriter means you have to take on board a lot of information and then re-write it in a creative and engaging manner that a voice over artist can read and a camera crew can film, always with the pressure that there's an entire production crew waiting for you to finish your work before they can begin their's. Anyhow the poetic writing had began to come back again. Gary had just got engaged, so here's one I wrote to commemorate the event. It is a bit tongue in cheek, it's called "Young Love".

Young Love
"You've got to get me in the mood,"
She said to me one night
You've got to talk me into it
I'm meant to put up a fight

You've got to woo and charm me
You've got to say you care
You've got to do a damn sight more
than shove your hand up there!

You've got to wine and dine me
and seduce me with your wit
you can't just blow inside me ear
and grab me by the tit

I want it to be proper
I want it to be nice
I want for us to get engaged
and save up for a house

I want to plan me wedding
and start me bottom draw
you can stop drinking with the boys
You can't see then no more

and you can't go t'match on Saturday

*we're going into t'town
we're off to chose some furniture
and put your money down.*

*You'll have to buy a decent suite
and get a better job
you'd better smarten up a bit
me dad thinks you're a slob*

*But meanwhile, for the moment
I really couldn't care
cos now that we've become engaged
you can shove both hands up there.*
Graham Rhodes

It might not be literature but it was what the audience wanted, anyway I've always been a sucker for a cheap laugh. I was also beginning to get a reputation of being outspoken. It was in this particular venue that I developed my opening line of -

"It's shut the fuck up time at the bar!"

Sometimes I wonder how the hell I got away without being punched. This was another popular poem I performed around this time.

Kill....
*All it would take is some bullets
and civilisation is saved
a few expert fingers squeezing the triggers
and then we can dance on their graves.*

*Let's plan the assassination
of the people we can't really stand*

Television celebrities, pundits and hosts
who are all so incredibly bland.

Let's gang up on Richard Whiteley
Shoot Paul Daniels and Debbie McGee
Anthea Turner; Noel Edmunds
and everyone from M.TV

Let's go on a hunt for Bruce Forsyth
kill Richard 'n Judy, then wait
for Nick Owens, Ann Diamond, Dale Winton,
but especially that cow Paula Yates.

Let's all unite as a nation
stand shoulder to shoulder and slay
everyone starring in Neighbors
and all them in Home and Away.

Euthanasia for Bernard Manning
Shoot Terry Christian on sight
Robson & Jerome, that kid from Home Alone
death is too good for that shite

But the two who deserve endless torment
two sons of the black Demon spawn
are the whining gits Foster and Allan
two blokes that should never been born.

But one bullets gotta be silver
on its mission it's got to succeed
cos Michael Portillo is Damien
the son of the Devil's own seed.
Graham Rhodes

It's a strange thing but I have a feeling I might not get away with that poem these days. What's even more scary is that a lot of the people I've mentioned in that poem are now dead, there again it was written over thirty years ago. I would like to add that I really don't have a problem with any of the people mentioned, with the exception of Bernard Manning and Terry Christian!

Whilst I continued in the late 90's working with these York bands I also ventured up and down the country by myself. I did two television appearances on a comedy stand-up show broadcast by the Daily Mirrors "Live-TV". I had to travel down to London for them, they weren't great and I'm not sure how many people actually watched either the show or the channel. For me the best part of the day was getting a free lunch in the Daily Mirror staff canteen, twenty four floors up Canary Wharf, a great subsidised meal eaten looking out over the great panorama of London.

I also had a poem read out on the television. On Channel Four's Racing programme! I still occasionally perform it today. It's about a personal hero of mine, the Irish steeplechase jockey Ruby Walsh. I think it was read out at a Cheltenham Festival meeting one year. Nothing came from this TV exposure. I don't think the man himself even heard it, but I was chuffed at the time.

Ruby Gets His Head In Front
You can hear the horse thunder
From Galway up to Nass.
The colours of the jockeys,
Emerald Ireland's sacred grass.

You bet and watch your money
drop in the bookies sack.
But Ruby's got his head in front

and gives the mare a smack.

*Some run just for money,
some just for the criac.
But when Ruby has his head in front
You'll get your money back.*

*County Kildare's bravest son.
His father bred him true.
He won the title at first try,
with Papillion he flew.*

*Three countries daunting Nationals,
all in the same year.
When Ruby gets his head in front
it'll cost those bookies dear.*

*From Gowran Park to Sligo,
Fairyhouse down to Cork,
you can see the bookies swagger,
you can curse them as they talk.*

*I lost my shirt at Wexford
won it back at Leopardstown
cos Ruby got his head in front
and brought those bookies down.*

*Some run just for the money,
and some just for the craic.
But when Ruby gets his head in front
You'll get your money back.*
Graham Rhodes

    I also performed at the Edinburgh Festival. I got a booking for two nights. The first in the Festival Club at 2.00am in the morning and the second supporting Earl Okin in a small Edinburgh theatre.

Unfortunately I never made that one. I was drink spiked just before going on stage at the Festival Club. The gig was like a bear pit. The audience, mainly drunks, had just thrown everything in reach, mainly beer mats and festival programmes, at a young band that did their best to play under the circumstances. I remember someone showing me the way backstage who also offered me some pills. I refused. I've always considered the offer of unknown pills as a sort of Russian roulette, I just don't do them. The next thing I know is that just as I was stepping out onto the stage, the stage manger whispered into my ear the immortal words –

"Don't forget this is the place that broke Jo Brand!" Cheers mate!

The gig itself was a bloody nightmare. As I attempted to speak people up in the balcony dropped the festival program onto me. I hit my shoulder. The thing was the size of a London telephone directory and it bloody well hurt! The roar from the audience was deafening, no one was listening. I struggled on shouting my lines. Nothing, then the drug kicked in. At first I felt dizzy, then I felt sick, then I began to feel paranoid. Suddenly it was as much as I could do to stand up. I held onto the microphone stand and looked out at the audience. It wasn't quite as bad as that scene in the movie "Fear and Loathing in Las Vegas", but it was getting that way. I remember picking up the mic stand, complete with mic and shouting at them –

"My name is Graham Rhodes. If you don't like it you can all fuck off!"

Then I flung the mic, complete with mic stand into the audience and walked off stage. My next memory is of being held by the throat by the stage manager.

"I don't care what you do to the audience, but you don't throw my gear around!" he hissed into my face.

I was beyond caring. With a swirling head I found my way out of the venue and found a cab that took me to the place where I was staying, a university campus. I had a horrendous night. I spent most of it sweating and shivering and hearing voices that weren't there. The first thing next morning I ordered a cab to the station and caught the first available train back to York. There I got another cab, got home and went straight to bed. I stayed there for the next two days laying under the sheets thinking, fuck Edinburgh and fuck drink-spikers, evil, nasty, underhanded excuses for people.

Once recovered and back in York, Gary and I decided to run a once monthly special night, a night mixing rock bands with comedy. We called it "Rock with Laughter". We had some great nights. Each month I acted as MC and did a poetry slot. We found some upcoming wanna be, stand up acts, and had an acoustic act as support. Life Support played the main, top spot. The first years shows were held in a York venue down by the riverside, almost on Skeldergate Bridge called The Bonding Warehouse.

I had played this venue before when a local musician called Liam Davison who had a Pink Floyd like band, the brilliantly named "One Stoned Snowman", staged a few psychedelic happening nights there. In 1995 Liam joined a guy called Bryan Josh, who also played at The Roman Baths and a few other York venues, and together they formed a band called Mostly Autumn. I never supported them but did see them a few times as they grew in both stature and number. They became what I suppose is a "prog rock/Celtic rock band". Now they are massive on the continent and to date have released thirteen studio albums and countless live albums. They have had many line up changes but still continue to this day. Liam Davison left the band in 2014 and in November 2017 Mostly Autumn released the very sad news that Liam had died. A sad loss.

The mid to late nineties was a great period of live music and good bands playing in and around York. As well as Gary Barrett and Life Support and Stone Cold Sober, Aldo's Orphans, the Surf Sluts, Mostly Autumn, and Hardlines there was also Zoot and the Roots, The Goosehorns, Shed Seven, Accidental Tourists, Breathe, Rory Motion, Benson, The Butter Mountain Boys, and Chris Helm, who one day was busking and playing the local gigs and the next day he was main stage at Glastonbury alongside Johnny Marr with The Seahorses.

The first night of "Rock With Laughter" was excellent and encouraged our plan to do it on a regular monthly basis. One night a few guys from the video company I wrote scripts for turned up and filmed one of the events. It turned out really well. I've still got the video somewhere. They were good nights and we got a regular audience. Then after a few months the Bonding Warehouse had to close due to refurbishment or water damage as every time the river Ouse rose the place flooded and we moved the club to a pub in Gillygate. Oddly enough the new venue was never as popular. It was at this venue that I met a young lady who wanted to be stand up comedienne. Her name was Catherine Stokes and week after week she would get up and deliver her act, which week by week got stronger and stronger. I did my best to encourage her to the extent that she used to call me her comedy dad. Now a farmer somewhere up near Cumbria, she still does.

In order to publicise the Rock With Laughter gigs, I used to pop into BBC Radio York every week and invade their Friday night "What's On" programme, which, back then, was hosted by a

Radio York presenter and Ian McMillan now better known as the Bard of Barnsley. Today I follow him on Twitter, but I don't think he realises that I'm the bloke that used to visit him at Radio York.

I got to know a few people at the BBC and managed to wangle myself a radio series on the ghosts of North Yorkshire, that I researched, wrote and broadcast myself. It was a fun project and I met a lot of people who were very sure that they had seen something that they couldn't explain. Among the people I talked to were the landlords of two pubs who claimed that their public house was haunted. One, The Saltersgate on the Whitby to Pickering Road, was supposed to have five different ghosts, and I believed the landlord. He was an ex-Barnsley pit deputy and they are the type of men not prone to over imagination. That was the pub that had the legend concerning the fire that was meant to never go out, and had two salt ovens, to dry the salt that was smuggled across the Moors from Robin Hood's Bay. Unfortunately as I write this, the pub seems to be in a constant state of disrepair, bordering on falling down, which not only is a great pity but an act of cultural and heritage vandalism.

The radio programmes seemed to go well and Radio York commissioned me to do a second series. However after the second series I ran out of locations and people willing to talk. Still I think twenty four ghost stories was pretty good going, especially as I was very careful to make sure I vetted all the contributors and, as far as I could tell, all of them believed that they had witnessed genuine sightings.

One band we booked at Rock with Laughter a couple of times, both in the Bonding Warehouse and in the Gillygate pub, was a young indie band from Middlesbrough called Velma, a four piece with a female vocalist. They should have made it much bigger than they did. Then a band came all the way down from Glasgow to play. They were called Seahouse. They did some original punkish rock material and a killer cover version of the Sex Pistols "Pretty Vacant" track. Somehow, and to this day I'm not sure how it happened, the bloke that managed them proposed putting together a tour of both bands, Velma and Seahouse, myself as MC and poet and Catherine Stokes doing her stand-up act. He assured us that accommodation and transport would be sorted, and the package would be paid each night for the gig, and the money divided out. After a while it was all arranged. I think the itinerary was York, Scarborough, Middlesbrough, Tain, Inverness, Aviemore, Fort William and Penrith. In the English towns Velma would get top billing, in Scotland it would be Seahouse.

From what I can remember the English gigs went well. Then we went into Scotland, to Tain. That must have been one of the longest car journeys I've ever taken. We English completely underestimate just how big Scotland is, especially when you travel as far North as Tain and Inverness. It took most of the day. When we arrived, around 6.00pm, we discovered the venue was half pub and half Indian restaurant. Not only that but they didn't want us to start the show till around eleven o'clock, and there wasn't a closing time, we were to finish when we finished. On the plus side, in addition to our fee there were free drinks and a free Indian meal for us all and bed and breakfast. We ate, we drank, and we did the gig. The bands went down well, but the audience weren't too sure about an English poet and female comedian. As Seahouse finished the night off another band arrived. They had played there the previous night and had gone on to another gig but their accommodation was screwed, so they came back to Tain hoping to find a bed for the night. Luckily enough there was and so a jam broke out. I'm not sure what time it finished but I staggered off to my bed around 4am and it was still going on then.

The Avimore gig was in a modern bar. Among our audience was a group of hippy travellers. During the gig they offered me a joint and afterwards I found myself disappearing from the bar into the surrounding woods where they were camping. We sat around a fire and chatted and smoked and when dawn broke it found me sitting on a rock in the middle of the River Spey watching salmon rise and deer come out of the woods to drink from the river. It was at that point that I seriously considered running away with the travellers. Then I remembered I had a show to do, a dog waiting for me back home, and the fact that I actually liked a comfortable bed at nights. Anyway I didn't do romantic poetry! I jumped from the rock to the river bank and found my way back to the chalet where we were staying.

The next couple of gigs came and went. Then, on a Saturday afternoon we arrived in Fort William. That was after a long drive down the Great Glen right alongside Loch Ness and Loch Lochy. It was at Fort William that we realised although our lodgings were there, the gig was in a place called Caol about four miles away. I sensed something was wrong when we arrived and began to off load the gear. As we dragged it into the bar we got sworn at for getting in the way of the giant projection screen showing the afternoons racing. As we set up I realised we in some sort of working men's club and that we were not their usual sort of entertainment. That evening I stood on the stage and introduced the show as follows –

"Good evening, this is the Rock With Laughter Show. We've two bands, a poet and a comedienne for you. We know you really don't want to see us, and that the booking is some agents idea of a laugh, but unless we play we don't get paid, so I suggest you go into the other bar and we do what we have to do and when it's all over we'll meet up for a drink. Please welcome the first

band...Velma!"

After I left the stage I walked to the bar. There was a pint and a whiskey waiting for me. I looked up at the barman. He nodded.
"That's for you. That was the most honest into I've ever heard!"

The gig itself went OK. A few locals ventured in and at the end, as Seahouse did their version of "Pretty Vacant", and the whisky flowed, to everyone's delight a drunken, hunchbacked gillie in plus fours, full tweed jacket and a hat adorned with fly's and fishing hooks attempted some sort of wild highland pogo.

The next morning as we were being served our full Scottish breakfast the landlady asked where we had played. We told her.

"Oh that place. A man was murdered there last week. He was found behind the bar with an ice pick in his head!"

As the sound of dropped cutlery echoed around the room she poured out more coffee and left us to it. To this day I've no idea if she was telling the truth or winding us up.

We did another gig at a club in Ayr and then Seahouse left us in Glasgow while the rest of us made it safely back to England to perform our last gig in Penrith, a late afternoon pub gig in front of a load of bikers. We went down great, in fact it was probably the best gig of the tour. It certainly was for me. During my set I'd jokingly made reference to a lack of dope. As Velma played I went outside for a breath of fresh air where I was hailed by a couple of bikers. They'd made a collection among themselves and handed me a fistful of joints. Wow, who says advertising doesn't pay!

The tour had been a moderate success. The bands had played

well and Catherine was further down the road to becoming the stand up comedienne she wanted to be, and I'd done what I always did, only to a Scottish audience. The downside was that the guy who put the tour together fucked off to Brighton with all the money. The only consolation was that we'd paid our way as we went. We left no debts behind us. In effect it was a free holiday with food and booze thrown in. Still it would have been nice to have seen for something for our efforts other than the experience!

I did a couple more gigs in Scotland outside of that tour. For some reason a manager who had put together a Stones Roses Tribute band that I supported and MC'd at a charity gig in Scarborough liked what I did and invited me up to his place somewhere near Glasgow, Cumbernauld I think it was. He got me a support spot to a band from Glasgow called Hugh Reed and the Velvet Underpants who, to continue the joke had released an album called "Take a Walk on the Clydeside". I loved them, you can probably find some of their tracks on "You Tube".

Yes we're now in the nineteen nineties. We now have home computers and are beginning to communicate via e-mail and finding new and exciting ways of promoting ourselves. I had a small basic web site, more for my script writing work than my poetry, and I had a rather splendid My Space site. Remember My Space?

Anyway I did a gig in a club in Falkirk where the acts were separated from the audience by a three to four foot high brick wall. Mind you it didn't prevent some arse from throwing a pint over me. Hey ho, being me I took it as a challenge and jumped onto the wall to shout my most insulting poem straight back at him. Don't let the bastards get at you. Despite dripping head to foot with the local brew I think I won the brownie points for having the balls to do what I did. I think between myself and the audience we settled for a draw.

Over the years I've handled many hecklers. There's no standard way to do it. Every heckler is different and so every response has to be, especially as it's of the moment. I've heard John Cooper Clarke say the immortal words "I can't hear you, you're mouths full of shit!" Bob Williamson's "The last time I saw a mouth like that Lester Piggott was sat behind it." To another folk artist who I've forgotten that simply asked "Is your village missing an idiot?" Personally I've gone into the audience and handed a heckler a mic before now. That has been known to shut them up. The heckler is the one reason a performer, especially a spoken word poet, has to remain sober until after the performance. If you're drunk or stoned and your thinking is a bit slow and you get a heckler you're toast. You need to be alert of what's going on around and in front of you. You need one eye on your poetry and another on the audience. Unless they are brilliantly funny audiences soon get bored with the heckler, usually because they are drunk and boring. Always remember you have the advantage, you are the one with the microphone.

I did one other gig in Scotland in the South West at Wigtown, Scotland's national book town. .Wigtown is a gorgeous place but a pig to get to on public transport. When I arrived I was staying in a pub on the main street and discovered I was appearing in a venue squeezed in between Melvyn Bragg and Kate Adie. Looking back I was the wrong poet in the wrong venue. They should have put me on in a pub supporting a local band, but no, this was a literary festival and I was put at the end of a large room with a seated audience. I survived. No one booed and at the end of each poem I received polite applause, but to me it just didn't feel right. For a start I sat down, a mistake. I hadn't sat down since the days of Krax. On the rail journey back home I thought long and hard about it and came to the conclusion that I'm a stand up, walk about poet, sitting down somehow takes the urgency out of my performance. To this day I still prefer a hand held mic so I can walk about and engage with the audience, to me sitting down just puts another barrier between me and them. Twenty or so years on and I'm still kicking myself for sitting down that night.

Meanwhile back in York I was still doing regular gigs with Gary and his band. We did a couple of out of town gigs, and then he got one at a biker rally, for MAG (Motorcycle Action Group), a motorcycle riders' rights group founded in 1973 to protest about the newly introduced motorcycle helmet law, but over the years it has expanded into many aspects of motorcycle operation in the UK. MAG currently says that it –

"...campaigns to protect and promote motorcycling and the interests and rights of all riders, from learner to advanced. We celebrate biking and the freedoms and independence it provides, through our support of parties and rallies, sport and competition, touring and travel".

Well back in the mid nineties they certainly knew how to party. None of us knew what to expect, especially as the gig was further up the A1 in deserted open country. We all had a certain sinking feeling when we passed through a police cordon that was around three or four miles from the actual camp. The site itself comprised a large marquee with a number of other, smaller tents pitched around it, all in a large field that was churned up into mud by motor cycle tracks. The bikes themselves were parked up in lines, none of them were small and all of them were powerful. Behind the main tent was a John Smiths beer tanker with pipes leading from the vehicle and disappearing into the back of the tent. We drove around the rear of the tent where the organiser was waiting to meet us. Much to our surprise he paid us in advance., I pocketed my money and wandered around the site while the band unloaded the gear and began to set it up on a stage inside the marquee. I hadn't wandered a fee feet when someone approached me.

"Want to buy some gear?"

Of course I did. The deal was done and I ambled back into the main tent for the quick sound check and to watch Gary and the band do their first set. The stage was positioned to one side of the main marquee, a bar ran along the opposite side and a great central pole, more like a tree trunk, was in the middle holding the whole thing up. The entrance was opposite the stage, as was a lighting rig. A DJ sat at one side of the stage playing a selection of heavy rock tunes. The audience, around a hundred or so, was already inside the marquee, mainly standing around the bar area. Some were at the entrance and some leant against the large tent pole. They were all dressed in muddy jeans, with shirts and leather waistcoats, leather jackets and motor bike boots. One glimpse at them and the word "biker" screamed out at you, in fact they looked like the bikers the Hells Angels had rejected.

The band came onstage and started their set. There was no reaction from the audience. That shocked me. I'd seen Gary and his band many, many times and I'd never seen them go down badly. They always went down well. They worked their bollocks off for the first half and still nothing. I walked to the backstage area as they finished their first half to a smattering of applause. As I stood there Gary walked past and just shook his head. The organiser noticed me.

"What do you do again?" He asked.

"Poetry" I replied.

"Jesus jumping Christ – you'll die out there!" he remarked helpfully.

He genuinely was worried for me and suggested I didn't go on. Gary who was standing near to me agreed.

"Sorry!" I replied. "I've been paid and can't give the money back, I've spent it on grass! I'll have to do the gig."

Gary and the man both sighed.

"I have an idea!" I said.

I went up to the DJ and asked what the audience's favourite record was.

"Alice Coopers "Schools out!" Came the reply.

I nodded "Right here's the plan. Play the track and put the spotlight on the central mic. Sometime during the track I'll walk out into the light. When the track ends I'll begin my set. When I walk away from the mic play the track again and kill the light."

He nodded. It was a plan. He began playing the track and a spotlight hit the mic. I walked onto the stage. As I moved into the light I began to roll a very large joint. It got the bikers attention. They began to shuffle and murmur and look at me. I made sure that they could see it was a real joint packed with real grass. I rolled it up, put it in my mouth and lit it. Then I took a really deep draw and blew the plume of smoke into the spotlight just as the track finished. I leant forward and spoke into the microphone.

"Right let's talk some fucking poetry!" I said.

I've no idea what their reaction was as I began reading my first poem, then went onto the second and before I knew it I'd finished my set. I stepped back from the mic and "Schools Out" blared out once again. I couldn't hear any applause but before I got off the stage a large figure strode towards me. It was the bikers leader. He was a giant dressed in a leather waistcoat and a kilt. The odd thing was he was wearing little zip up slippers, just like ones granny used to wear. He was called "Bear". I knew that because he had the word tattooed on his forehead. As he approached me I remember thinking that if he hit me it would be so hard that I wouldn't feel a thing, I'd be out cold. He didn't hit me. Instead he gave me a massive bear hug that lifted me off my feet and squeezed the air out of me. Then he kissed me full on the lips and turned to his fellow bikers.

"Poetry!" He proclaimed.

The audience shouted the word back. Before I knew it a chant of *Poetry, Poetry Poetry,* rang around the tent. He dropped me and I gave a little bow and left the stage.

"You lucky bastard!" Gary muttered as I walked past him.

He and the band returned to the stage. This time they were met with applause, the second half went down amazingly. As soon as they hit the first chords the bikers began to dance. As the set progressed the dancing got wilder and wilder. At one point I found myself on the end of a long line of bikers being whirled around and around. Further into the night I found myself on top of some bikers being pushed up the main tent pole. It was a wild night, fuelled by Gary and his band and John Smiths beers. On the way back home I rolled a joint and reflected that I had taken poetry where poetry had never been before, and survived.

I did another biker gig, only this was something special. I've no idea how I got it or when or where I was approached but Scarborough was, and still is famous for motor bike racing with its iconic Oliver's Mount track. In 1995 the organisers decided to stage a series of gigs (I hesitate to call it a festival), over eight days and nights at a stage set up where the visitors to the races would be camping. The whole thing went under the title of Scarborough's International Bike Week. There was the stage, a lot of concession stands, and a bar. However the site was some distance away from the actual Oliver's Mount track, as I discovered when I first arrived. In fact the site was nearer to Seamer than Scarborough, it was next to a landfill site near to where Morrison's supermarket stands. I knew it was near to Morrison's because at lunch time, every day for eight days, a member of the crew would disappear and return with one cooked chicken and a bag of fresh doughnuts for all crew members, myself included.

Oddly enough when it came to on-stage I was classified as a crew member, but when it came to overnight accommodation I was left to my own devices and stayed in a bed and breakfast place in the Old Town of Scarborough, run by a crazy saxophone player called Baz Hampshire who, late into the night, would drink whiskey with me and tell me tales of playing saxophone with Little Richard and Jerry Lee Lewis. Baz had retired but had once been a journalist and had been co-opted to help in the creation of a couple of books written by a man called Chas White better known as Dr Rock, Scarborough's rock and roll chiropodist (I kid you not! I believe his radio programme is still broadcast by BBC Radio York), they were the biographies of both rock and roll legends and had involved him travelling to America to meet and talk to the two men and, in Baz's case, to join their bands. Baz also led a popular Scarborough band called Hamp's Tramps that played a sort of comedy jazz, and played at the biker week gig. I was pleasantly surprised at his place, waking up each morning, albeit with a headache, to the sound of seagulls and a view of the harbour and the South Bay. I was less pleased when after three days I realised the organisers were under the impression I was paying for the accommodation myself. After a heated row I was reassigned to sleep with the crew in an untidy and shabby lodging with three to a room. Once again it was the case of someone somewhere in charge of the purse strings thinking that MC's and poets not only worked for nothing but enjoyed paying their own money for the joy of working for them. Hey, it's only rock and roll!

The actual job was tougher than I expected. Each day I'd walk onto the stage at twelve o'clock, make a few announcements and introduce the first band. This went on until five o'clock when there was a break before the whole thing kicked off again at seven o'clock until midnight, and repeated itself for eight days. Unfortunately as the bike races were on at the same time, and that the organisers vastly overestimated the crowds love of live music, I usually walked onto the stage at twelve o'clock and made announcements to the flock of sheep in the next field, the herd of cows in the field beyond that and a few pissed off stall holders who had paid good money to stand in a deserted field leaning on their stalls waiting for customers.

The evenings were busier audience wise however I had to start the proceedings by announcing the results of the day's races, including accidents and fatalities. From what I remember there were two over the weeks racing. What I don't remember is the name of many of the bands I introduced. Let's face there were a hell of a lot of them, and not all of them were local. I can remember Bandana, because I befriended them. There was a band called The Tadpoles, who had a musician with one eye. He told me the gruesome story of how he lost it. He was fishing off the rocks on the Marine Drive at Scarborough when someone standing above him, up on the Drive itself cast his line. The hook flew down and hit the guy in the eye and pulled his eye out. Even writing this causes a little shiver to run down my back.

There was also a great Goth Metal band from Nottingham who, for the life of me I can't remember their name, who were on the same night as the most spectacular act and the person that was on the top of the entire festival bill, albeit it was the Wednesday night, the legend herself Suzie Quatro.

Despite the fact she wasn't due to perform until 10.00pm she arrived early in the afternoon, and spent most of the time sitting in the backstage area challenging members of her band and anyone else who passed by, to play backgammon. She was quiet, soft spoken, unassuming and friendly dressed in a checked shirt and jeans. A couple of hours before she was due onstage she disappeared into her dressing room, a small Portakabin.

I did my usual job of announcing and introducing the evenings bands, and doing my own ten minute spot just before the main act. Throughout the evening the audience numbers had built up and by the time my spot arrived it was a pretty full house. I looked up and realised I had never performed to so many people before. I carried on as I had every night, almost the same banter and the same poems. As usual once the audience got over the surprise of seeing and hearing a real live poet on the stage they enjoyed what I did. Mind you, every night this had been an audience of anything from one to two hundred. This Wednesday night there must have been at least five hundred going on a thousand. Looking out all I could see were people, most of them dressed in racing leathers. It was packed. Certainly the stall holders made their money that night. As usual I finished my set on a poem called "Road Rage" dedicating it to every biker there. As it ended I raised my arm and held my hand in a clenched fist and lowered my head and a wave of applause washed over me. Then the wave got bigger. I heard a voice coming out of the PA.

"Look up!" It said

I looked up. The lighting guy had somehow turned the lighting around so it was on the audience. I was being cheered and applauded by the largest crowd I'd ever performed in front of. I stood there for a moment or two and drank it all in. It was like having a warm shower. Then I remembered I had a job to do. I invited them all to carry on clapping and cheering and egged them on. Then I announced Suzie Quatro and the cheering went up by at least ten decibels. I left the stage as she and her band walked on.

She performed for almost an hour. An hour of high level rock the like of which I've rarely witnessed. It had been pre-arranged that I would thank her and bring her back on-stage for an encore. I made the announcement and as she returned onto the stage I walked passed her. I noticed her eyes. They were enormous; I swear to God that they looked like the eyes of a bush baby. Then she kicked off on a twenty minute version of her hit, "Devil Gate Drive." I had never been a fan before, but I was now. She was absolutely brilliant. The epitome of rock professionalism. It was a privilege standing on the same stage to witness it all so close up.

The eight days came and went and I returned home. It had been long and tiring. It had its highs and lows. The worse low being the morning that the backstage Rottweiler attacked Ben, my border collie. My girlfriend at the time had come to visit and brought him along and had left him with me whilst she had gone off to Scarborough. As I walked him by the front of the stage this bloody great beast suddenly appeared from backstage and attacked.

I quickly yanked Bens lead pulling him away from the Rottweiler's teeth. I repeated this action about four or five times and was beginning to panic as I knew there was nothing else I could do, when an observant member of the crew who had spotted my dilemma drove up in a car with the back door open. I knew what I had to do. As he slowed down I bundled my dog into the back seat and followed him slamming the door behind me. We drove off as the puzzled Rottweiler looked after us. I saw its owner come along and drag the beast back stage where it lived in a large cage. Later that day he apologised. He had received a right telling off as the dog had been in a public area, but claimed he had no idea how the beast had escaped and promised it would be chained up for the rest of the week. For the rest of Ben's life he carried the scar tissue along his back where the dog had bitten him.

It must have been due to that series of gigs that I began to get requests to host charity gigs at a venue in Scarborough called the Pavilion Vaults or the PV as it was known locally. It was a night club in the basement of a 1960's office block, a terrible bit of architecture that replaced a rather elegant older Victorian building that used to be the Pavilion Hotel. There was, and still is, a greasy spoon type cafe opposite and I used to catch the train out of York and get there early so I could have one of their all day breakfasts before descending the stairs to discover who and what I was about to introduce. A couple of York bands played these gigs, I know Hardlines did at least one, but mainly they were local Scarborough bands. At the end of the day I would catch the last train back to York.

Somehow I landed a gig in Bradford supporting the one and only John Otway. I was excited for a number of reasons. Firstly it was a paid gig, secondly it was supporting John Otway. I loved that guy. I had a number of his albums dating right back to the late seventies when he emerged from the post punk scene in a duo with Wild Willie Barrett. If you have no idea who this man is get hold of You Tube and check him out. He has a crazy and unique way of delivering his songs. Thirdly it was in Bradford giving myself and my girlfriend an opportunity to have a real Bradford curry.

The gig itself was in a converted swimming pool, Wilson Baths I think it was. I should really check that out as I have a huge poster of the gig with my name on it, autographed by the man himself tucked away somewhere. In fact come to think about it I've loads of posters of various gigs I've done that I've always wanted to get framed and hang on my walls. I just never seem to get around to it.

Anyway I arrived at the venue, checked the time of the sound check and disappeared off to the Indian restaurant where we had arranged to meet another couple, a girlfriend of my girlfriend and her boyfriend. We met up, ordered our food and were given the poppadoms and pickle tray. We were well into the Cobra beers when I realised I wasn't going to have time to eat my meal. I explained to the waiter what was happening and he kindly arranged for it to be put into take-away boxes so I could eat it at the venue. I made my apologies to the others and left them to enjoy their meal. When I got to the venue I left the cartons in the dressing room and went out onto the stage to do a sound check. Now it doesn't take a lot of sound checking for someone with my act. I'm one person needing one microphone with a small amount of reverb. Total sound check time? About five minutes! However in that five minutes John Otway had arrived and was shown into the dressing room. When I arrived back he was halfway through eating my curry.

"Excuse me, that's my curry!" I exclaimed.

"I thought it was my rider!" he explained.

"No it was my curry, paid for with my money!" Was my answer.

I did my opening set and seemed to go down alright. At least no one threw anything at me and they laughed and applauded in the right places. His set was brilliant and once the curry incident had been forgotten he turned out to be a really nice bloke. After the gig we hung around and had a few drinks together. That was when he signed the poster. It turned out he was as hard up as I was. That was why he signed the poster with the words - "I write scripts too!" I've always hoped our paths would cross again, but they haven't.

Back in York I was booked for a gig supporting another York band, the very wonderful psychobilly surf band The Surf Sluts. It was for a private party. The aunt of the lead singer Fez was getting engaged and, as she and her partner were both fifty years old they thought it deserved a party. They'd seen me perform and wanted to commission a poem to commemorate both the event and being fifty. As I began the writing process it dawned on me that I too was approaching fifty, and as I began to write the poem, it became more and more autobiographical and personal. I called it "Now we're pushing fifty!"

Now We're Pushing Fifty
Now we're pushing fifty
We should wear our age with pride
We've been there and we've done it
And we took it in our stride

We bopped to Little Richard

With Elvis had our first kiss
Back row in the movies
A grope in the one and six

A tanner in the juke box
A fiver for your pay
Riding with Gene Vincent
On the back of a BSA

The Beatles brought us Strawberry Fields
The Stones the Altmont Blues
And war movies on all TV's
The latest Vietnam news

One two three four
We didn't want that fucking war
But what can a poor boy do
Cos sleepy London Towns no place for a street fighting man
Chilly, chilly its evening time
And Waterloo Sunsets fine
When I think of all the good times
I have wasted - having good times

We lost a few along the way
Jimi & Janis couldn't stay
Tim Buckley and Jim Morrison
Sang their song and passed along

But we who still are standing
We who still survive
We've been there and we've done it
We wear our age with pride

We wear it like a banner

We are the ones who dare
We're growing old disgracefully
We're fifty - and we don't care!
Graham Rhodes

I've been performing that poem now for over twenty years. After my own fifties it became "Now We're Pushing Sixty". Then It became "Now We're Over Sixty". Recently it became "Now We're Bloody Seventy!" Hopefully one day I'll walk onto a stage to proclaim "Now We're bloody Eighty!" Let's see.

As I was now fast approaching fifty my own birthday party was arranged. As it happened the day fell on a Thursday, the same night as Gary and his band played their weekly residency at York's Roman Baths pub. I assumed it would be an ordinary night, it wasn't. Gary and his band played the first bit of the night, various solo singers including Tony Jackson who was a regular at both Rock with Laughter and the Roman Baths, played a quick set and then the band Hardlines turned up and joined in. At the height of the evening I was presented with a birthday cake. Not just any birthday cake. It was a birthday cake made in the shape of a Gibson Flying V guitar, just under life size. It was a work of art in cake and icing and had been specially commissioned from a York shop named Imaginative Icing and created by a man who went by the name of Captain Ants. Spectacular, a great way to enter my fifties.

There was another special birthday at the Roman Baths. This time it was for a lady called Rita who had reached her sixties. As a fan she had supported all the local bands and had attended most of the local gigs since God knows when. She had her own special place in all the rock pubs, but didn't go to Fibbers because she couldn't afford it on her pension. A special night was arranged for her and people asked me to write and perform a poem in her honour. It was a great night and here's her poem, bless her.

Poem for Rita
She rules the whole scene
She's York's rock 'n roll queen
She's seen everyone
From stars to has been's

She started shaking with Gene Vincent
rattled with Marty Wilde
rolled to the Swinging Blue Jeans
she took to dancing in the aisles

she did the twist to Chubby Checker
and jeepstered with T Rex
hopped with Mott the Hoople
to the Eagles she had sex

she glammed up with David Bowie
wore tinsel with The Sweet
got heavy with Led Zepplin
and boogied with Canned Heat

she's boogied with the best of 'em
Thin Lizzy and Status Quo
Play anything by Bad Company
And watch Rita go go go

She knew young Gary Barrett
When he was in short pants
She even knew old Aldo
When he was nobut just a lad

She knew all of the Hard Lines
When they were just soft curves
she joins in all their choruses
she knows all of their words

Our York's a ghost filled City
There are spirits near and far
Of Vikings, Normans, Romans,
There's spirits behind Bars

But there's only one that shines out
Like a beacon to us all
And that the spirit of our Rita
The true spirit of rock 'n roll
Graham Rhodes

I was still doing the occasional gig at Fibbers, and was especially chuffed to be on the bill supporting the wonderful Half Man Half Biscuit, four boys that shook the Wirral, as their publicity claimed. I was sandwiched between The Surf Sluts and the headliners. As four blokes the Half Man guys were pretty nondescript. They were polite and unassuming. It was only when they began singing their songs that you realise just how subversive they really are. I mean anyone who comes up with the concept of "Joy Division Oven Gloves" is an absolute genius. As a writer I've always loved the wit and inventiveness of their lyrics, especially their song "All I Want for Christmas is a Dukla Prague Away Kit." An absolutely brilliant take on fans buying football shirts. In my humble opinion their song "It's National Shite Day." should be our new national anthem. I was really glad to see them perform live, let alone share a stage with them.

I was also asked to support to the one man I had spent the last twenty or so years being compared to, the bard of Salford himself, Mr, (now Doctor), John Cooper Clarke.

We met in the dressing room well before the gig time, chatted, and chatted some more. Eventually he offered me some chemicals and I introduced him to Theakston's Old Peculiar. Then we had some more chemicals and some more beer. By the time Tim

Hornsby (The owner of Fibbers) arrived to tell us it was show time we were both very much worse for wear. I went out and did the worst set I think I've ever done. Turning two pages over at a time, getting lost in my most familiar poems, it wasn't brilliant. Then John Cooper Clarke came out and did his contractual forty five minute gig in less than twenty minutes. It was so short that Tim made him go back onstage to fulfil his full forty five minutes. God knows what the audience thought about it. When we parted we shook hands and decided it would be better for both our careers, and health, if we never gigged together again.

What was he like? Well he was personable, witty, great with words and anecdotes and not the healthiest person I'd ever met. At that point in his life he was thin. I know he always has been thin, but he was even thinner. He had a slight shake and his teeth had a slight green tinge to them. He spoke with a nervous stammer. I liked him as a person and even got him to autograph a book of his that came free with one of his early albums, "Snap Crackle and Pop".

Tim must have forgiven me because sometime later I appeared at Fibbers once again. This time supporting the Surf Sluts at the launch of their album called "Pot Sounds". This time they pranked me. Just as I walked onto the stage they tipped a bin load of talcum powder over my head. I walked on regardless in a swirl of white powder that was picked up by the lighting, creating a rather interesting effect. Every time I moved my head another white cloud swirled around me. To the audience it must as looked as if I was on fire, or at least undergoing a heavy smouldering.

I was also booked to play the Knaresborough Festival once again. Someone had decided to revive the idea of an arts festival in the town and call it "Feva" (Festival of Entertainment and Visual Arts). I hosted an all day rock gig in a pub called The Market Tavern, and did my stuff between acts. Among the many acts I introduced was an excellent little psychedelic band called The Purple Mushrooms that I liked a lot. The following year, in addition to hosting the rock gig, I also did a reading at a pub called The Borough Bailiff where I topped the bill at something called "The Dead Good Poets" night. The pub was always a favourite of mine from when I lived in Harrogate, especially as it used to be open all day on Knaresborough market day. Unfortunately the last time I was in the town I noticed it had closed down. I sincerely hope that it reopens sometime in the future as it was a rather excellent pub.

The gig was rather good as for once I was in the company of other poets. Gigging with bands I don't usually get to see many other poets perform and I remember sitting at the back of the room being surprised at the range and quality of their work. That's not meant to sound condescending. Up to that night, with the exception of John Cooper Clarke I don't think I'd seen or heard another poet perform for God knows how long. I was a pleasant and refreshing change for me, and reminded me that I quiet like other peoples poetry.

That particular year Roger McGough was also performing at the Knaresborough Festival. Unfortunately I was unable to go to his gig but I was introduced to him one evening at a small bistro. He had just finished his meal and I joined him for a drink afterwards. We sat a bit bemused and did the polite chatter thing. He had just published his book "Bad Cats" and offered me a signed copy. I exchanged a small booklet of my own poetry that I had managed to self publish and sold at gigs. Amazingly he remembered Krax magazine and the poems he contributed. We parted after half an hour with a warm handshake.

In my non-poetry world writing was taking up more and more of my time and I was approached to do some writing for a guy called Tony Mallett, a journalist working for the York Evening Press who had just set up a free magazine aimed at the York pub goer called "Up For It!". I contributed a weekly column called "Opinionated" which was basically a rant against anything I wanted to rant about. My brief from Tony was to be contentious. I fulfilled it as best I could. In fact it was so contentious that I wrote it under a non-de-plume. After a drunken meeting with Tony I came up with the name Zercon Mercedes. Most editorial meeting were drunken, as all of them began and ended in a pub. Well after all it was a pub based magazine! We figured that Zercon Mercedes was probably the ultimate glam rock name we could come up with. We were joined at the magazine by two other writers. One was called Bill, who lived just outside York in some sort of farm where bands like Benson rehearsed, he wrote the movie reviews and occasional articles. The other contributor was Anthony Springall, better known as Captain Ants, who lived in Scarborough and reported on the music and social scene on the East Coast. As well as being on of Scarborough's most intriguing eccentrics, Captain Ants was, and still is, an amazing cake maker working at a company called Imaginative Icing, and yes it was that very man who had created the amazing the birthday cake for my 50th birthday.

Whilst I was still living out in Tockwith I had started gigging with another band that I'd met at one of the Scarborough gigs. They were called Bandanna and played a great series of cover versions, especially their version of the Cranberries song "Zombie". They gigged at various pubs along the A64 and at one in Boroughbridge.

I was taken to their gigs by a youngish man who was a fan of both myself and the band. He was a maniac driver and scared the living shit out of me every time he drove me anywhere. He stopped taking me when he got involved with another Tockwith resident, a guy called Dave Codling who was a musician and artist and who used to play guitar in the 60's band Quintessence when he was known as Maha Dev. I saw Quintessence a couple of times back in the day, once at Leeds Town Hall and once at Leeds Poly but I'd never really got into the Indian mystic thing so I never followed them. Anyway the man turned up in Tockwith, inheriting his mother's house after she'd died.

In addition to painting and occasionally playing guitar, he also used to deal in certain illegal substances. He was an alright guy and I enjoyed spending time talking art and music with him. He had graduated from Leeds Art College in the early 60's and post Quintessence, had lived and worked in Hollywood returning to Tockwith in 1995. He accompanied me to the Roman Baths and played there a couple of times. However, once he started dealing heavily I didn't like the people he was associating with and so I dropped out of that particular scene. As I was writing this book I read that the man had returned to America where, sadly, he died in July 2019.

Recently I bumped into Andy the old leader of Bandanna who now plays in a Scarborough based band called The Hummingbirds. He told me that the guy who used to drive me to the Bandanna gigs also died, sometime around 2000, not unsurprisingly it was in a car crash!

As I've already mentioned I was now as a full time scriptwriter for a couple of Leeds based production houses and was going out with a female lawyer called Lynda who introduced me to one of her clients, a guy called Darren who was working in the newly emerging computer games industry. He owned a small development company in Knaresborough and commissioned me to do a few bits and pieces of writing for him, mainly scenarios and dialogue for the games he was trying to develop. Then he got lucky, he was head hunted by a major games publisher. I didn't hear from him for a while until one day he contacted me. Would I like to write the dialogue for a game being developed in Germany? It was a role playing, space exploration game and if I was interested could I go to Dusseldorf the following week. Too bloody right I was interested!

A week later I found myself in an office in an industrial estate on the outskirts of Dusseldorf meeting with a production team headed by someone called Bernd, the games inventor. I sat and listened to the games concept and looked at the moving images, characters, worlds and races they had already created. It was a sort of empire building game, the player could trade and build up their own little empire, or could just trade and explore. In theory the game could go on forever should the player be content to travel and trade. At first I felt overwhelmed, but over the next couple of days I began to get a handle on it and wrote some sample dialogue and came up with some game ideas. They liked what I did and we agreed a monthly fee. By now the internet was fully functional and so I worked remotely on the project from England and would visit Dusseldorf whenever it was necessary, which as it worked out, wasn't as often as I had originally hoped. The deal was struck and in celebration the production team arranged to take me for a night out in Dusseldorf before I returned to England.

The first place we visited was a "traditional" German restaurant where they ordered something called a "meat platter" for me. This was a huge platter filled with every type of meat you can imagine, and some you can't! Steaks, chops, sausages, things that looked like burgers, bits of meat I wasn't too sure about. It was a platter of meat put together by an over imaginative butcher. Sensing it was some sort of test, along the line of "sink the Englishman", I set to and managed to eat the lot, more out of sheer, grim determination rather than appetite. By the time I'd finished I felt like meat was oozing out of every pore in my body. Then they took me to a traditional German bierkeller, traditional in the fact that it was either an old, genuine, pre-war building complete with original decor right down to the wallpaper and the wooden tables , or a complete reproduction of one. It was just like the ones you see in the movies. It was a strange sensation but I felt uncomfortable. As I sat there drinking steins of beer I expected to see Christopher Isherwood sitting in a corner as young man dressed in lederhosen stood up to start singing "Tomorrow Belongs to Me".

It was in that bierkeller that I learned the unique method of German drinking etiquette. You sit there and waiters bring trays of drinks to your table. In order to keep score they mark the number of beers you've had on a beer mat. Before you have finished one drink there they are again with a tray full of fresh, full steins and make more marks on the beer mat. At the end of the night they total it all up and you pay. Civilised I call it. No queuing at the bar, no jostling, and no trying to catch a barman's eye by waving money in their general direction.

The last bar was the best. It was a rock and roll bar, surprisingly like Fibbers, only bigger and louder. For some reason a couple of the guys I was with warned me not to cause any trouble as the place had a bit of a reputation. We sat down and a tray of beer was brought to us. As the waiter slid the large steins across the table to us he looked me up and down.

"Hey, you rock and roller?" He asked in broken English

I nodded and before anyone could say anything he leapt onto the table.

"I am Germany's only Gene Vincent impersonator!" he proclaimed.

He then went into a version of "Be-Bop-A-Lula" in a strange quasi German-American accent. The thing that impressed me was that he even did the stiff leg thing. I sat there with my mouth open as he went through the first verse and chorus before jumping off the table and returned to his job of serving beers. I looked at the rest of the party. Their mouths were open as well. It turned out that they frequently visited the bar and had never seen that sort of behaviour before. One of them looked at me and shook his head.

"You rock and roller!" he simply said.

I was still smiling to myself when I boarded the plane home next morning.

The job lasted two years, and when it was finished it was published as "X-Beyond the Frontier" and was one of the first ever games produced for the Microsoft X-box.

The producer must have liked what I'd done because as soon as I had finished it I was signed up to write a second one. This one was for another independent games developer that had been funded by THQ, only this time it was being developed in Berlin. Once again I was flown out to Germany, this time business class with all the little goodies, snacks and free drinks that go with it. I was to meet the producer at Templehof airport.

Now to anyone who has never been to Templehof the name means nothing, but to students of German history it means a lot. It was originally built in 1927, but redesigned and rebuilt as a part of Albert Speers plan for the reconstruction of Berlin. Then main building was designed to resemble an eagle in flight and is such an amazing bit of architecture that Lord Norman Foster has described it *as "one of the really great buildings of the modern age."*

Unfortunately it will be forever tainted by the fact that it was Hitler's pride and joy, it's post war history makes for a fascinating read. Check it out sometime. The down side to Templehof airport is the descent and landing. The plane seemed to suddenly turn in mid air and make a dive towards the runway, leaving my stomach a few thousand feet in the sky behind me.

Once on the ground I had an interested encounter with the German customs man in charge of the metal detecting gates. In anticipation of the inspection I had emptied my pockets and placed my bag on the rollers next to the x-ray machine. I had even taken my bracelet and rings off. Still, as I walked through the machine, it buzzed. The guard looked at me. I realised I was wearing my black leather bikers jacket, covered in zips and buckles. Annoyed at my own stupidity I shook my head, gave a little sheepish grin, and placed it on the tray with my other belongings. I walked through the machine. It pinged again. This time the guard pointed towards my large metal belt buckle. Again I shook my head and slid the belt from my jeans. Holding my jeans up with one hand I walked through the machine and once again it pinged. Simultaneously the guard and I both looked down at my cowboy boots and the metal pseudo spurs wrapped around the heels. We looked up at each other. I shrugged and bent down and removed my boots. Once again I ventured into the machine. Once again it pinged. I was puzzled and looked at the guard. He pointed towards my shirt. I was wearing a denim shirt with metal press stud fasteners. I sighed and removed my shirt. Once again I walked through the machine. Nothing. I smiled and now on the other side I began to dress myself.

"Yah! You are metal man!" The guard said smiling as he handed me my boots and jacket.

The producer was waiting inside the airport and whisked me off into what he explained was the old East Berlin. He explained that when the wall fell a rebuilding process began in the centre of Berlin and worked its way outwards into the suburbs. Now almost a decade later the building work was still going on, and the production team were working from an office in a new building at the end of a street that had only been halfway modernised, the remains of old East Berlin were to be found at the end of the street. It was dusk as we got out of the taxi. I looked down the street into the heart, and memory and imagined the ghosts of East Berlin. I gave a little shudder.

The team I was working with were young and enthusiastic, their company was named after the game they had invented. It was called "Yager", German for Hunter, and they had been working on it for the last five years, prior to the arrival of the American games publisher who had come along and thrown money at it. We talked and they trusted me to put a voice and character to their creation, a pilot called Magnus Tide. I worked on that job for over four years and, in my opinion, wrote some of the best dialogue I've ever written. I gave the hero an edge, and a back story. When it was published back in 2002 this is what three reviewers said. –

The characters come alive in Yager. There are 20 you interact with, in varying degrees. Voice-acting is well done -- you're frequently contacted by friend and foe alike on your ship's comms and humor is liberally laced throughout. I often found myself chuckling at some of the things Magnus and the other characters said. Script writer Graham Rhodes contributed to Yager's storyline. Magnus will sometimes remark, "Whatever happened to Graham Rhodes?" ***http://tarasresources.net/yager.htm***

"Sound is very good in terms of ship and weapons sounds and background music that varies with theme and tempo. There are 20 characters you interact with, voice acting is very good with some well-done foreign accents, scripting and humor.

"Yager is funny! I often found myself chuckling at the characters wise-cracks. Yager is a sleeper!"

"Voice acting is excellent and time was obviously taken in the script writing. Humor is liberally laced throughout and I often found myself chuckling at some of the character's remarks, especially Magnus's sarcasm and wise cracks. One of Yager's biggest treats is its character-heavy storyline. Magnus meets up with technology-deprived Russian mechanics, free trade zone barkeepers and redneck outlaws, and all of them have something interesting, funny or silly to say."

On the box and in the insert, under my photograph the guys at Yager just credited me as Graham Rhodes – Poet.

One night in Berlin Darren, the producer, and I were stumbling from bar to bar when we decided to investigate the streets of old Berlin where we invented a game loosely based on the movie "Funeral in Berlin" which as far as I can remember comprised the pair of us jumping in and out of darkened doorways saying the words *"My names Michael Caine!"* until we got bored and found our way back to the hotel. Not much of a game, I admit, but I guess you had to be there.

The joking was fine until one day I had lunch with one of the members of the production team. He told me that all the original Yager team had been born behind the wall in East Berlin, and all of them remembered life there. Christ, you get a whole different perspective on stuff when you talk to the people who were actually involved. The guy I was talking to was the oldest of the group and hence had the longest memories of living in East Berlin. He had actually lost a friend who had been shot whilst trying to escape to the west. Not for the first time in my life I thanked my lucky stars I am who I am, and was born where I was born.

Once again I worked remotely on the project, each week sending another chapter of the adventures of Magnus Tide across to Berlin, whilst most discussion about character and chapters was conducted by e-mail. I think I only got to visit Berlin twice more. One of those visits was especially memorable.

It was morning and, as you do when you're abroad, I was getting dressed watching Sky News. I wasn't paying much attention until with a shock I realised that I was watching a picture of Leeman Road, the end of my own street back in York. It was underwater. It then switched to a picture of Kings Staith, showing the usual York flood picture of water flowing in, out and around the famous riverside pub. I turned the volume up in time to hear someone say that it was the worst flooding York had experienced in years and, as the water came down from the Dales, it was expected to get worse. I made a couple of phone calls and within the hour a flight and taxis had been arranged. I also made a call to my local York cab company; yes they would meet me at Manchester Airport and take me back to York. That night I was back home in Leeman Road, working alongside members of the Army, council workers, and other residents, helping to lay sandbags around the endangered houses in the lower part of the area.

The River Ouse stayed at full flood for two or three days. On the Sunday I walked around a eerily quiet city. I took a look at the huge metal flood gates under Lendal Bridge. It was scary knowing just how much water was being held back, and what devastation would be caused if they gave way. Gary Barrett and his band were playing a Sunday afternoon gig at the Bay Horse pub on Marygate. I walked across Lendal Bridge and through the Museum Gardens to take a look. Halfway through the gig I wandered down to the bottom of Marygate and took a look at the flood defences. Three layers of sandbags were on top of the huge metal gates. I scrambled up to see just how high the river was. It was running less than half an inch from the top of the uppermost sandbag. I looked back up the road to the pub and made a mental calculation.

The level of the river was actually above the downstairs rooms of the pub. If the river burst Gary and his band would be playing underwater.

It was whilst I was living in Leeman Road that I found I was getting a bit bored of York. I know that seems a bit of a ridiculous statement, but in my real job as a script writer, over the years I'd lived there, I had written the history of York about six or seven times. It started when I created the audio-visual display at an attraction called "The York Story" that used to be behind the Jorvik Viking Centre. Then I revised the script when it was made into a sell-through video. Then I was approached to write scripts for other videos about York. All of them kept the wolf from the door but I was going over old ground. By now I knew all of York's little secrets.

Like the fact that the shrine of St Margaret Clitheroe in the Shambles isn't really the house she used to live in, that house is two doors further up the street but wasn't available to purchase when they decided to create the shrine.

Like the fact that no one knows which is the real Cromwell's death mask, as when copies were made, someone got the original mixed up with the copies.

I also know where to find the rear of an original Norman house and know of the rumour that the Anglo Saxon city of York was found under the Redfern Glass site but not explored as someone was wanting to build a hotel on the site.

I also know that the famous Viking helmet wasn't found on the Coppergate dig. It was found hanging on the prongs of a digger operated by Wimpy and was off the main archaeological site. Speaking of the Coppergate dig, way back in the seventies when Neil Simone and I had a gallery in York, I bought a brass reproduction of a Viking Torc, a bracelet that was being sold to raise funds for the archaeological dig. Since then, with very few exceptions, I have worn this bracelet on every gig I have ever done, I still do. Over the years it has become my lucky charm. I always promised myself that when I made it I would have one made in gold. As yet I haven't!

I was constantly annoyed that, when all my York scripts were sent off to various historian and experts, they came back with comments saying things like, "You can't say that. You have to say "It might have happened. Or it could be that..."

Eventually I learnt that no historical expert would ever say that something categorically happened. They would never nail their colours to the mast. They were and still are, too afraid that someone, sometime in the future will come up and prove it didn't happen like that. As a script writer it drove me crazy, but I had to put up with it. After all I was getting paid to write it.

Eventually I got so fed up of it that I decided to write my own York history book. It took me around a year but by using my own research and putting in the historic material I hadn't been able to use in the video scripts, and by making up a whole load of fictitious history, I created a book called "Footprints in the Mud of Time." The title being a paraphrase of Longfellow's poem "Footprints in the Sand of Time."

The book is a comedy history, a mixture of outrageous truth and lies and when reading it the game is to identify the two. I put Gary and his band in there, I also put Aldo's Orphans in as a medieval band of strolling minstrels. I'm in there as a Victorian performance poet who jumps out at people in the street shouting his poems. You can probably tell I had a laugh writing it

I made a deal with a York printer where he would print the book in return for a percentage of the sales. Once again

Waterstone's were very helpful in providing me with a shop window and a book launch. For the next couple of years you could find me walking around York with a bag full of books supplying local book and tourist shops with copies that they sold. Tony Mallet reviewed it and came up with a nice line that we put on the back of the book -

"Reads like Terry Pratchett got drunk with Bill Bryson and together they attack The City of York."

The introduction of the book was written by the York Member of Parliament of the time, Hugh Bayley. He did it as a favour after I'd read a couple of poems, acting as his warm up act, in a public meeting on the back of a truck in Rowntree's Park when he was standing at a general election. One of the poems I read was an anti-Tory poem called Eighteen Fucking Years.

Eighteen Fucking Years
They couldn't sort a piss up in a brewery
but for eighteen years they've fucked with you and me
those Westminster alcoholics with their bloody gin and tonics
really did screw up our economy

For 18 bloody years they've held the power
and shat upon the British working class
they stitched us up and sold us down the river
so let's all united and knock them on their ass.

For far too long we read about their scruples
the ones they say that should apply to us
whilst they drift to Chelsea flats to screw their mistress
enjoying the privilege of class.

*Let's not forget the crucifixion of the miners
the railway workers and the poorly paid
and the selling off of water and the systematic slaughter
of the unions that our fathers fought to gain.*

*For eighteen fucking years they screwed the country
and made riches for their families and friends
with beneficial policies and market force economies
and told lies about their assets and their wealth.*

*So when it comes to voting, you do it wisely
vote green or loony, or whatever is about
vote anything you bloody well have to
and get those sad Tory fuckers out.*
Graham Rhodes

Hugh Bayley was so pleased with it that he asked for a copy and later claimed he made copies and passed them around Westminster. To this day I don't know if he did, but it's a nice story and I like to think it's true.

Anyway back to "Footprints in the Mud of Time." I managed to sell around five hundred copies of the little book. It didn't make a fortune but did well enough to encourage the printers to do a similar deal with another book idea of mine. It was a series of my drawings of York all printed up in a book that was a reproduction of a sketch book. I got the printer to bind it with a metal spiral binding along the top and a sheet of tracing paper between every page. It was expensive to produce and although we sold a fair number of copies the project only just broke even. There was no more self publishing for me until Amazon came along a few years later. Speaking of which "Footsteps in the Mud of Time" is once again available in both paperback and kindle versions with a nice new cover, via Amazon of course.

One of my last gigs in The Roman Baths was supporting Gary Barrett and Life Support on New Year's Eve 1999/2000 at the millennium, end of the century gig. I was still going out with the lawyer at the time and she had booked a room at Thomas's, the York hotel right opposite York Minster so she and her nine year daughter could hear the bells and see the celebrations. I stayed with them for a while before dashing across to the pub to deliver a poem to see in the new millennia. This is it –

Millennium Poem
Happy new fucking millennium
Lest drink till well all bloody burst
Lets drink to the future
Lets drink to the past
And prey that things just can't get worse

Happy new fucking millennium
Lets drink to the next thousand years
Lets drink to the hope
Lets drink to the glory
Lets drink to an end to our fears

Happy new fucking millennium
Lets drink to a golden new age
So throw on your glitter
And chuck up 'yer bitter
And drink to us turning a page

Happy new fucking millennium
Lets drink as the big wheel goes round
Let's all stay at home
And not visit the Dome
What a waste of a few million pounds

Happy new fucking millennium
But so far I see nothing has changed
We're still just as poor
National health's at deaths door
and Labours gone fucking deranged

Dads Army is still on the telly
they still haven't legalised dope
Man U's won the league
The workers still bleed
New Millennium, new Labour – same old joke
Graham Rhodes

As I was saying, I was getting tired of York and decided to move. A number of factors were making my mind up. The main one was that my parents who lived in Hunmanby, a village near Filey on the Yorkshire coast, were both now in their nineties and wanted to see a bit more of me.

Another factor was that the East Coast Main Line had just announced that the London to York rail service was running a direct train that made the journey between the two cities in less than two hours, hence the property prices had just shot up.

A third reason was that I had a manic neighbour who was making my life difficult by repeatedly breaking into my kitchen and sitting in my sink! The first time it happened was surprising. The second time annoying, and by the time it happened for the fifth time it was just plain infuriating, especially as he was a hard bastard, useful with his fists and usually out of his head on a cocktail of legal and illegal drugs and alcohol. He'd been arrested so many times it was a joke. The York police now avoided him as trying to arrest him usually ended up with at least one of them getting hurt. One day he shouted through my letter box that there were paedophiles living in the street. He did this for over half an hour before wandering off. He was really pissing me off, especially as, at the time, I was writing the dialogue for the Alan Hanson Football computer game against a tight deadline. That night I typed the word Scarborough into a search engine and pressed the key. The next day I put my Leeman Road house up for sale.

Chapter 5
Scarborough
2001 - 2019

I arrived in Scarborough in the late spring of 2001. At first I rented a top floor flat up in the Ramshill area of the town. Then with the grace of an understanding bank manager who gave me a mortgage, I bought it. It took me a little while to get used to the novelty of living by the seaside. I was still writing the script for the Yager game and writing various business to business scripts, but along with my dog Ben I found the attraction of the sea alluring. Every morning I would leave my flat and walk down the cliff, through the Italian Gardens, let Ben off his lead and follow him down to the old ruined South Bay swimming pool and onto the beach. Depending on the times of the tide we would walk around the remains of the old pool to the Spa where would catch the cliff lift and return up to the Esplanade and my flat, only to discover that half the day had gone.

Poetry wasn't at the forefront of my mind but I was asked to perform at the Knaresborough Festival once again, this time supporting John Cooper Clarke. Despite saying we would never gig together again, there was no way I could refuse. I had a new lady friend now who grudgingly agreed to drive me there and back, but it was pretty obvious to me that she didn't think much of the idea We got there with little time to spare and I managed to met John Cooper Clarke a few minutes before the gig started and we just had time to exchange a few words. The gig was at a venue called Henshaw's Arts and Craft Centre in a large room that must have seated around a hundred or more people. I remember walking onto the stage area, taking the mic in my hand and hanging my leather jacket onto the mic stand. I did a full set of thirty minutes and left to a really appreciative round of applause. I stayed to watch John Cooer Clarke but as my lady friend wanted to get back to Scarborough, I didn't even have the chance to have a post gig chat and drink. All the way home along the A64 she made it very clear that she didn't want to get involved in such antics in the future.

As I settled down to a seaside way of life I went along to an amateur theatrical performance up at Scarborough Castle. It was a specially written, one man play about and starring, Richard the Third. It was long, too bloody long, but the actor was amazing. I had no idea, and still don't know, how actors manage to memorize their lines. I've tried to memorise my own poems and fail miserably at that. I need the security of that little bit of paper that holds the words. You'd think that after performing some of them hundreds of times I would be able to read them off without the paper, but somehow my mind just goes blank. I just can't do it. One reason is that whilst I'm up there I'm looking at the audience and listening to what's going on, so I can make a comment and draw whatever's happening into the act. Sometimes I might pause in a poem to make a comment, and I need the paper to get back into the poem.

Anyway back up at the Castle, I chatted with the guy organising the theatre group, Henry, a strange, round little man with white hair and beard. He looked like a typical theatrical and when I told him I was a writer he listened. Back then his group was called the Crossfade Theatre Company and they did one or two plays a year. I began to write for them and turned out a number of short, thirty or forty minute plays that his little troupe gamely performed. Then a couple of the female members approached my lady friend and reported the organiser of conducting some sort of sexual harassment. He was a bit odd I have to admit. We went to a party at his house, a wooden place at Reighton Gap, which turned out to be some sort of druidic wedding where he officiated in front of old standing stone he claimed to have dug up and relocated into his back garden. Personally I wasn't too sure about that. If he had relocated an ancient stone it was cultural vandalism, if it wasn't an old stone he was lying to the couple he was "marrying" . He claimed he talked to his cats in Rumanian, he also claimed he was Johnny Kidd, as in the singer in the late 1950's early 1960's band Johnny Kidd and the Pirates. I once challenged him about this, citing the fact that Johnny Kidd had died in a car crash back in 1966, to which he just winked and said it was a tax avoidance scam. As he was plainly lying I didn't bother pointing out that if he really was Johnny Kidd he must have shrunk about a foot in the intervening years. Anyway after the sexual harassment accusations were made a meeting was held, with the result that he was asked to leave the company and, more by accident than design, I found myself in charge of a small amateur theatre company.

We did a few performances in Scarborough's rock pub Indigo Ally. One of the performances there was a memorable performance by Captain Ants who had returned from New Zealand the previous year and was planning to return. His performance was meant to represent this return journey. Although he knew what he was about to do, his entire performance was improvised. He walked onto the stage area dressed in a souwester hat and an old oil skin and began to blow up an inflatable dinghy. He then handed out to the audience bottles of water, spoons and pots of yoghurt. He then took out a mechanical toy seagull, placed it on his head, and asked the audience at the key words "waves" and "seagull" to throw water and yoghurt at him as he sat in the dinghy narrating his story of his journey to New Zealand. By the time he had finished Captain Ants and the stage area of the pub was dripping in water and yoghurt. Graham, the landlord, told me it took three weeks to get rid of all the yoghurt. It was one of the funniest, most abstract, surreal theatrical performances I've ever seen.

I think the company ran for three or four years. We moved from Indigo Ally to a pub at the other side of town in Valley Road called The Valley. We performed one night a week, on a Thursday and did serious plays, comedies and pantomimes, whatever I felt like writing really. We did two performances in Dalby Forest on behalf of the Forestry Commission; we also did Halloween ghost walks.

We even did two summer seasons on the Scarborough Pleasure boat the "Regal Lady" where we performed a Ghost Ship two nights a week, playing to a couple of hundred people every night. I donned on a Goth leather coat, heavy make-up and frilly shirt and played the part of the ghost vampire narrator who, spitting fake blood, gave the spiel to the audience and introduced the other actors (dressed as ghosts) who told the story of their own grisly demise. I used to address the audience from the upper deck, at the head of the staircase, and when the sea was rough, almost got pitched overboard on more than a couple of occasions. The script I wrote for the performance made use of three or four real Scarborough ghost stories plus some I made up for especially for the occasion. Oddly enough, some years later, a Ghost Walk appeared on Scarborough front. Its route around the Old Town took it past the house I lived in. It used to stop just outside the front window and I always gave it a listen. Imagine my surprise when I heard the narrator tell the tale of one of the ghosts I had made up for the Ghost Ship!

The little company also played the Ilkley Literature Festival and won a couple of awards at The All England Drama Festival staged at Saltburn. The number of performances and the things that happened within the group and the interactions between members, not to mention the plays themselves, could fill a book in themselves. Unfortunately Michael Frayn has already written "Noises Off", so that's out, but you get the idea.

Sometimes if we were short of actors or if a play wasn't ready, I would stand in and perform a set of poetry. It usually went down well with the exception of one of the actors, an elderly lady who used to be a professional actress and had appeared in a couple of soaps. She hated my poetry and once even threatened to leave the company if I ever performed them again. In her defence she used to say I was a better writer than that. In my defence, the material was, and still is funny and audiences still like it, and there was nothing else to fill in with.

Eventually the theatre company had to move from the Valley Pub as it was being refurbished and they wanted to extend the restaurant so we moved to a small arts centre on the edge of town. It was the kiss of death. Our audience just didn't want to walk that far, and the place didn't have a bar. I think we stayed there, hanging on for a year before I left. In an attempt to get an audience we had added a singer songwriter to the mix, to perform a twenty minute set between plays. It didn't really work but I did get to meet some of Scarborough's excellent singer songwriters, including a young political singer called Joe Solo who was originally from Hull and had been a singer with a punk band called Lithium Joe. I always smile to myself when I look back at his gigs with us. The first was during a play of mine about Scarecrows and the First World War called "Potters Field". Joe had and still is always been a student of the First World War and shortly after he wrote and released an album called "Music from Potters Field", then "Going Home, Music from Potters Field PT2."

I am constantly amazed at Joes persistence and dedication both to the history of the First World War and to the people who died there. Since 2011 Joe has committed himself to a creating a Facebook Group that lists every single soldier from Hull who died in the First World War. It's called The Hull Pals group check it out sometime, it's an awesome undertaking.

Here's a link-
https://www.facebook.com/groups/341367989231888

A bit later I wrote a small play about the Spanish Civil War called "Spanish Knights", and the Joe supplied the in-between plays performance. Shortly after Joe produced an album about a lorry driver from Hull called Jack Atkinson who went out to fight in the Spanish Civil War called "No Pasaran!"

As the writer of the theatre group I also invented a number of comedy characters that could act as fill ins between plays. There was Lord Richard Ramswriggler, a down at heel aristocratic sheep farmer whose wife was having an affair with her personal trainer and who was constantly at war with the weasels that infested his farmland.

Then there was Ruby and Mabel, two old ladies that featured in three different comedy plays.

There was Sockman. A character that was simply an actor's hand in a sock that ranted and raved about the state of the world in general.

There was also Ned Foremandale, a pastiche of an actual man called Fred Normandale, a successful local fisherman who owned five trawlers. His character would stamp onto the stage dressed in full oilskins and yellow wellington boots, wearing a mayoral gold chain from which dangled a wooden golden fish and shout at the audience his catch phrase "You're not eating enough fish!"

I attempted to get BBC Radio York interested in the characters and met up with a presenter called Jerry Scott who did a midnight programme from their Scarborough based studio. He liked the idea and passed them on, but the powers that be weren't too keen and nothing happened, apart from the fact that on certain nights of the week I would pop into the Scarborough studio where Jerry would put me on air to chat about music and play a couple or three tracks. Back then it was Western Swing that I played him.

However the two best theatrical characters were two poets I invented. "The Revolutionary Poetess" and a character called "Blodwyn Pygg".

The "Revolutionary Poetess" was brilliantly played by an actress called Soraya Marr. She came onto the stage dressed basically as Che Guevara complete with Doc Martins and a black beret. We only did the act a few times, but the most successful one was at a festival in York organised by my comedy daughter Catherine Stokes. She asked me to MC the day and in return I managed to get a spot for this character. Soraya stormed onto the stage and delivered the poetry in such a believable way that the audience actually believed she was for real. This is her act –

The Revolutionary Poetess
Walks on stage to the Clash "I fought the Law."

Makes clenched fist salute-

                        Right on – sisters,

in a quieter voice

                        …and some brothers!

I'm going to start with a homily to vegetarianism. I call it - "Who Kills the Cows"

*We kill the cows to eat the meat
And turn their skin to leather
We buy the jackets in a shop
To protect us from the weather
Then - we kill each other to steal the jackets*

Society you are sick!

*Or is it us,
that is sick of society?*

Thank you.

Some of you may be laughing now, but tonight as you lay sleepless in your beds, think how our society jails people who protest for animal rights – and finds nothing wrong with spending Saturday afternoons in high street shops called The World of Leather!

Tongue sandwich's yuck! It's been in something else's mouth!

Here's another on the same tack

	Meat eaters are gastric fascists
	Eating fish is just the same
	Fish have eyes and heads and feel pain
	Crabs and shrimps have mothers too!
Pause	
	Thank you. Short but very much to the point! Have you ever noticed that we only eat animals that are herbivores? Chickens, sheep and cows don't eat other animals – well not unless the animal feed companies put it into their feed when no one's looking. Mad cows? They're bloody raging!
Shakes head in sadness	
	Onward and upward -
Looks up to audience	
	This one is called - Food is a Sexist Issue
	The world is as round as a pizza ...as round as a McDonalds
	as an apple
	But sausages and bottles of coca cola

> *are shaped like penises*
> *even the food on my plate is a*
> *sexist issue*
>
> *I sour my fish with vinegar but it's*
> *you wearing the chip on your*
> *shoulder*
>
> *Bastard!*

Looks at someone in audience

> What's the matter with that?
>
> Listen mate - during the class war your mother knitted socks for soldiers.
>
> My mother wore them - don't start!

Pulls herself together

> I'm sorry about that
>
> No I really am - After my last poetry reading I promised myself I would try to be less confrontational.
>
> Well actually I promised the police sergeant, that bloke from the fire brigade and my probation officer.
>
> To this day I still say it wasn't my fault.

I never expected the Finchley Young Conservatives to take me so literally. As I said in court - if they couldn't face the truth they shouldn't have booked me in the first place.

Talk about shooting the messenger

She gives a shudder.

Talk about bad karma!

Talk about revolution – and I am!

This one is dedicated to the downfall of capitalism …and in particular, my overdraft

It's called Revolution

You say you want a revolution
Well you know we all want to change the world
You tell me that its evolution
Well you know
We all want to change the world
But when you talk about destruction
Don't you know that you can count me out

Unless it the destruction of the York branch of Barclays Bank and it's bloody manager
The Fascist pig!

Thank you – that one's very dear to my heart.

So's this.

Marx once said all ownership is theft – I agree with him – so if the person that took the right side front wheel off a Fiat Punto parked outside please return it – we'll say no more about it.

I'm not joking – unless the thief brings it back, I'm stuck. I can't get home tonight

Anarchy's OK but it's like charity – it should start at home –

Pinch your own wheels scum-bag.

I'll leave you with this biblical quote.

It's from Acts chapter 26 verse 14

And when we were all fallen to the earth, I heard a voice speaking unto me, and saying in the Hebrew tongue, Saul, Saul, why persecutest thou me? It is hard for thee to kick against the pricks –

> It's the story of all our lives – especially mine!

Gives raised fist salute

> Keep on keeping on!

Leaves the stage.

END.

God I loved her. She deserves a revival, if anyone reading this would like to take her on just get in touch.

Then there was the other poetess. I called her Blodwyn Pygg although she started off life as Ophelia Bottomley. She underwent a name change when the actress who played her, a talented lady called Karen Tite, decided the character should be Welsh, so Welsh she became. I know that Blodwyn Pygg was actually the name of a late 1960's band led by Mick Abrams, a guitarist who had left Jethro Tull, but the name sort of fitted. We both liked it and the character became very popular with our audiences. We even we took her out of the theatre to actual gigs. We entered her in a BBC Comedy Competition and she won, which was a bit weird because she beat me doing my own poetry act. Mind you I was surprised I got as far as I did as some years previously I had entered a similar competition only to get disqualified as the judges decided that poetry wasn't stand up comedy!

Blodwyn Pygg was actually based on a number of poets that I've come across in my life who perform their pretentious poetry in poetry society's and at poetry clubs up and down the country. They are the type of poets I dislike most of all. I suppose in some way she's my revenge on that entire poetry scene.

Karen really got into the character. She would walk onto the stage holding a knitting bag, wearing a long "hippie" type skirt with a crochet shawl draped around her shoulders with her hair up in a bun held in place by two wooden knitting needles. Here she is

Blodwyn Pygg
Theme music - Sham 69.

Walks on stage
(to the audience)

> Good evening friends and, dare I say the word … fans.
>
> Once again it must give you great pleasure to hear me say the now immortal words – Peace Love Drugs and Crochet .
>
> It seems that since my last performance there has been, what I can only describe as a fluffy backlash in favour of my more gentile, sorry I mean genteel, my more genteel style of poetry.
>
> So for your pleasure and delectation here's some more of my poems. The first one is called - "Dawn is a bright new beginning"
>
> …a good choice for the start of a poetry reading - even though it is evening now -
>
> Anyway not to worry - "Dawn!"

Dawn is as bright and shiny

As the smile of the clown

on a Mac Donald's Happy meal

like the smile on a face

of a favourite clock

heralded in by the

sound of a cock

a bright new beginning

like a sack full of shillings

hitting the pavement

It makes my heart sing

As I hear it all ring

And makes me want to

fill my pockets

with your loose change.

(Pause)

Thank you…

I hope you noticed that, in my references to coins I used the old coinage in a symbolic manner – representing Britain as it used to be - when it was Great, before all this decimal nonsense.

It was not, as some unkind people claim, a reference to my addiction to LSD – as in the hallucinatory drug.

And let me tell you, if any more scurrilous reports appear in the Sunday papers, about my alleged mind expanding experimentations they will be getting a letter from my solicitors – Messers Shaftem, Grabbem & Breakem, Limited

Here's another new one –

Appropriately it's a poem about fear.

It's called "Banging in the Night."

(Looks up)

I'm sorry, did someone say something funny?

No?

Well as I said, this one's called Banging in the Night.

The window keeps on banging
But I daren't take a look
The door keeps on banging
But I'm too scared to look
My pipes must have an airlock
There's noises in the air
I'd really like to have a peep
But I don't think that I dare

The wind outside is restless
There are noises in the night
I'm pulling up my sheets
I've had a nasty fright

Thank you.

Again I hope that you recognised the deep symbolism in the poem - where my comparison with having experienced severe wind problems during the night actually represents the way our society refuses to accept the fact that the numbers of homeless people are growing.

There really are too many people sleeping rough, the government should be opening more night-time soup kitchens.

(Drifts off to herself)

Oxtail would be nice – or maybe minestrone –

Or even a nice hot cock-a-leakie.

(Comes back to the present)

Where was I now – oh yes poetry. This next one is also all about man's inhumanity to man –

Well actually it's about man's inhumanity to one man in

particular.

OK, yes you've guessed it. To me!

It's called.

"How come you never phoned!"

Takes out a packet of tissues. Looks at the audience.

By the way, if after hearing this, anyone would like to avail themselves of a tissue, please don't be shy. Just form an orderly queue.

(Coughs)

"How come you never phoned?"

How can you share
the same thought
and not be one
how can you throb
to my being
and not belong
why did I start caring
about your pain
and lose interest in my own
was it because the
glass was only half-filled
and you poured the sparkle from
the wine
and your cheap cham- pagne
turned

into my real expensive pain.
(pause)
(shouts)
The least you could have done was ring - you shit!
(To audience)

Sorry that last line wasn't really in the poem. It was just in case the little… is in here tonight – call it improv…

That Andrew Motion does it all the time. I know I've seen him. I'm sure he makes half of it up on the spot. Well it does sound like it, doesn't it?

Anyway this next poem's dedicated to a much better poet. Once again the fickle finger of fate has swung pendulum like…

…once again it is appropriate to read verse written by that much lauded poetess and calendar maker extraordinaire Miss Patience Strong.

At last her endless pursuit of a thousand poems concerning nothing more challenging than kittens and balls of string as published by that wonderful female organ "The Peoples Friend" is being regarded as the major work of literature that it surely is. They must remain as an inspiration to us all.

I know they do for me.

This penultimate one is for her – once again it's both deeply meaningful and symbolic…I'll leave it to you to work out the hidden meaning for yourselves.

It's called "Kittens and String"

My neighbour had three kittens
I often watched them play
I gave to them a ball of string
They found them strangled
yesterday

Thank you.

I'd like to leave you with a final poem once again ladened with meaning and deeply symbolic…

But mainly irony, yes it's definitely ironic…

It's a cry from the past that echoes down all our futures.

Actually it's not one of mine.

The words scream down the years to us from a halcyon period of our history – inspirational words written by one of our greatest leaders of youth Jimmy Pursey, a wordsmith of such profound wit, emotion and intellect.

Please try to hold yourselves when you hear them.

Sorry, I mean hold yourselves back!!!!

Just take a look around you, what do you see?

*Kids with feelings like you and me
Understand him, he'll understand you*

*For you are him, and he is you
If the kids - are united -
then we'll never - be divided
If the kids – are united –
then we'll never - be divided*

*Hersham boys, Hersham boys
Lace up boots and corduroys
Hersham boys, Hersham boys
They call us the Cockney cowboys*

*Come on, come on
Hurry up Harry, come on
Come on, come on
Hurry up Harry, come on*

*We're going down the pub
We're going down the pub*

> A very noble ideal indeed! If I see you downstairs, mines a large one.
>
> Peace, love, drugs, crochet and, of course that gorgeous little Jimmy Pursey and Sham 69.

Bows & leaves stage.

END.

Once again, I love that character, as did the audiences. Again she's locked away in the external hard drive of my computer when she should be out there drifting onto some stage somewhere, and making people laugh. God bless her.

At the same time as running the theatre group I was also working with Captain Ants, who had decided to put together a Scarborough version of the "Up For It" magazine in a newspaper format. Tony our original York editor had packed the York version in and had taken a job out in Brussels as a real journalist writing for "The European". I wrote a whole series of articles about local bands, local events and general tittle-tattle. I think we ran that for around three years before it ran out of money and steam. Here's one of my typical articles, from an issue dated 9th Feb 2002.

A Reet Good Do! –

Thanks to everyone who made our Bar Staff of the Year awards such a success. We nearly died when we realised that you lot out there had cast over two thousand votes for your favourite bar person. Not only that, but the world must have been watching 'cos the next day we had over one thousand hits on our web site. Amazing, we never realised our little organ was so well read.

Our heartfelt thanks goes to our hosts Indigo Alley and all who sailed in her. Thanks also goes out to the many landlords and brewery reps who contributed the raffle prizes. We were miffed not to win the signed Paul Middleton CD, speaking of which, the man and his band played another knock out gig. As we keep telling you this band is seriously good. Paul seems to be in that act of redefining the Blues, transmuting it by adopting English lyrics and subject matter with musical influences from Capt Beefheart, Zappa, Howling Wolf and the Pink Floyd! Watch out for them when they play Scarborough again. God they're so good it's even worth travelling to Harrogate to see them on Thursday nights at the Blues Bar.

Not exactly Pulitzer Prize material but what is interesting is that we staged a gig that starred Paul Middleton, I'm pretty certain I read a couple of or three poems that night, which is sort of nice because, if you remember, Paul Middleton was a member of the Harrogate band Wally that I read poetry with back in the early nineteen seventies.

Scarborough has a great history of excellent local bands and performers. To celebrate this fact, in 2001 four young guys got together and staged a gig on the beach. It was called Beached and was a success. They did this the following year when Captain Ants and I recorded it in Up For It. The following year I was asked to host, and act as MC for it. I did and continued to do so for the next eight years until eventually through a lot of different circumstances it proved impossible to stage and Beached came to a halt. It was shame. Not only did it bring some amazing bands and acts to Scarborough, it also filled the beach with tourists for the weekend. The driving force was four young Scarborough men. Toby Jepson,

Steve Dickson, Steve Monkman and Mike Lynsky, however from what I remember a young guy called Tom Wotton who was at university back then, helped them to do all the required health and safety checks. However despite the gigs success, every year Scarborough Borough Council made it more and more difficult for the organisers to stage it. It was obvious to all that the leaders of the council did not approve of such an event happening without their own organisation having a hand in running it.

One year they got the police to try to stop it. I was a witness to this cack handed effort. It was the Saturday morning and a small group of uniformed officers came backstage and claimed we should shut it down as a flash flood was expected. That wouldn't have been so bad if it had been raining. It wasn't. The sky was clear blue and cloudless. When this was pointed out they then claimed that it was raining in Whitby. Someone got on a mobile phone and rang a friend in Whitby, it wasn't raining up there either. Eventually when the organisers refused, and knowing all the paperwork was in order and there was no breach of the law occurring the police gave up and went away.

Another year the council banned the audience from bringing their own alcohol onto the beach. The Friday night before the gig I was on the main stage with some of the crew. It must have been about midnight when we noticed little groups of people scurrying about on the beach. The lighting guy turned on the spots and lit the beach up. There were a number of people all busy with buckets and spades burying bottled and cans on the beach for the following day!

Then there was the year they decided to put a fence up around the bit of beach where the audience used to stand. To this day I'm not sure why, but the orange plastic fence appeared on the Friday night. Halfway through Saturday afternoon the tide went out and left the end of the fence high and dry on the middle of the beach, people simply ignored it and walked around it. You really do have to wonder at the level of intelligence of these people.

Over the years I introduced over a hundred acts onto the stage that looked out over a beach and the South Bay towards the headland, the lighthouse and the pier. Some were famous and some became famous. There was Frank Turner, Amy MacDonald, The Fratellies (Who got their vehicle stuck in the sands), The Foals, The Hoosiers, Nine Black Alps, Dodgy, The Enemy, Alabama 3 (The only band I went into the audience and danced to), The Lancashire Hot Pots, Thunder, The Call, One Night Only, Martin Stephenson, as well as a lot of local bands and solo performers.

Martin Stephenson provided an interesting episode in my life. When he played Beached he discovered that I was a script writer and asked me to write a play about a hero of his, an American musician called Charlie Poole, but before we get to that there's a little medical interlude to mention. The night after the 2002 Beached gig I got a pain in the chest. It turned out to be a heart attack and I was admitted to the cardiac unit of Scarborough Hospital. Once diagnosed I was lucky enough to survive and was nursed back to health by the brilliant National Health staff. Amazingly I seemed to get over it with no great problems, except they discovered I was type two diabetic, and I had to give up smoking! That lasted for five years until I made the tactical error of having a week's holiday in Amsterdam. Well, it was a case of "when in Rome", unfortunately it stuck and I regained the habit, mainly grass as opposed to just tobacco – hey ho!

I was fit and well by the time the next Beached Gig came around and remember walking onto the stage to make the first announcement wearing a t-shirt with an exploding heart motif.

"Sick bastard" someone in the crowd shouted.

"It's my heart!" I replied.

I always tried to make an effort for Beached. One year I bleached my hair white claimed I misread the invitation and thought instead of saying "Beached", it said "Bleached" – no, no one found it funny back then! Then there were the years I Gothed up. Goth Cap, frilly shirt and black leather coat. It was basically the same costume I used when I played the ghost Goth vampire in the Ghost Ship performances back on the "Regal Lady" ghost nights.

Back to Martin Stephenson. Having to take time off I managed to do some research on Charlie Poole. He turned out to be a fascinating character who was an alcoholic banjo player who made the first record to sell a million copies, a little ditty called "I'm the Man Who Rode A Mule Around The World." He came from North Carolina, hence the name of his band, The "North Carolina Ramblers". To give you an idea of his drinking capabilities, when he was asked what he needed for his first New York recording session he replied, *"A gallon of whisky and a dozen lemons!"*

I wrote the play and Martin, together with some friends of his from a Newcastle music club, the Jumping Hot Club, decided to stage the play. He would put together an American string band and I would put a small cast together to play the roles. I decided that I would start the play in a second hand music shop where two young musicians would see and laugh at a banjo and the owner of the shop would narrate the Charlie Poole story.

Meanwhile, on the opposite side of the stage, two women played the role of Charlie Poole's widow and his sister, this was set in 1936, just after the man's funeral.

Between them on the centre of the stage, was Martin's band who would interrupt the dialogue playing a selection of Charlie Poole's songs. It was staged over two nights at Newcastle's Live Theatre and was a sell out every night. Then the problems began. The money for the musicians was taken, as was the money for the expenses and the digs we had all stayed in for a week of rehearsals. The rest of the money was taken by the club to pay their own expenses and debts. This had nothing to do with the play and so the actors and myself never received anything for our efforts, not a bloody bean! Martin said he would sort it out but he never did. The money had gone. To make matters worse he had allowed someone to make a documentary featuring the band and glimpses of the play without checking the copyright or consulting with myself or the other actors, and once again, there was no mention of payment for our work.

Again I found myself asking why people expect writers and actors to work for nothing. Needless to say we fell out about it and have never spoken since. Hey ho, at least a play of mine got to be staged in a real theatre and my name is on the poster. Speaking of which, I'm a long time fan of an American singer songwriter and author called Kinky Friedman. I'd seen him in the nineties in Leeds and in York at Fibbers, and had a book signed by him. In return he had a copy of my York book. He played the Live Theatre the night before my play but, as we were knee deep in rehearsals, I couldn't get to see him. He did however autograph my Charlie Poole poster wishing me good luck. One day I'll get around to having it framed, alongside the John Otway one!

Meanwhile back at Beached and Scarborough a Japanese metal band was on the bill. They were called Electric Eel Shock. The first year they played they supported Thunder, who when they saw them, locked themselves away and revised their set. They returned three years later to top the bill and stayed a few days before the gig. Now what no one knew was that in Japan their guitarist Akihito Morimoto, known as 'Aki' is also a famous fisherman. He is a competitive angler and writes for Basser Magazine, Japan's largest fishing periodical. He spent three days on Scarborough's pier pulling all sorts of fish out of the sea, much to the surprise and amazement of the locals. When it came to the gig, halfway through he pulled a giant cod out of his gear and held it up to the crowd.

"Scarborough!" he shouted before throwing the fish into the crowd,

It was meant to be a goodwill gesture but unfortunately, as the story goes, it hit a blind guy in the audience and someone took umbrage and the dead fish hurtled back towards the stage at twice the speed it left. Meanwhile I was standing at the side of the stage oblivious to what was happening and to flying cods. Toby Jepson who was stage managing the gig saw what was happening, calculated the trajectory of the cod, grabbed me and pulled me back just as the dead cod whistled past the end of my nose and smashed in a heap into the drum riser. It is still one of the more memorable moments of Beached. Recently almost ten years later after their Beached gig, Electric Eel Shock played Scarborough once again and I met Aki. When he saw me he laughed and simply said "Cod!"

I made some good friends at Beached. Toby Jepson, one of the organisers and stage manager was the lead singer of the 90's rock band Little Angels. Over the years since they split up he had performed as a singer for Gun, Fastway, Dio, and a couple of other bands. He had also carved out a solo career releasing a few singles and EP's. He also became a successful producer working with Saxon, The Virgin Marys, Toesland, Chrome Molly and many others. He was one of the first organisers to leave, but he had a career to follow and unlike the others his career often led him out of Scarborough.

He has always been a huge supporter of my work and had me record some poems with an idea to actually make an album but as yet we've never got around to it. He asked me to support him when he played Fibbers in 2007, when he released the first of three EPs entitled "Guitar, Bass and Drums". He moved out of Scarborough a couple of years ago now, relocated down south and formed a band called the Wayward Sons that are enjoying a deal of success as a live band playing material from their debut album "Ghosts of Yet to Come". At the time of writing a third album is expected soon.

The Beached organisers were always looking for something new and one year they decided I should co-host the gig with a local comedian who ran a comedy club in the town. He lasted halfway through the Saturday before he ran down to a cheap book shop to try to buy a book of jokes. I don't think he turned up on the Sunday.

Then for two years I co-hosted the gig with an energetic young guy who went by the name of Jim Taylor, better known as Mr Jim. We hit it off immediately and, between acts, got the crowd to do all sorts of daft things. It took us a day to realise that despite our urging, the crowd couldn't bounce up and down as they were standing on sand! I think it was that year, at the request of a young helper dressed in his self-made dragon costume I got the entire crowd to sing "Spider Pig".

Jim was on hand at a difficult Beached moment. Earlier in the year Ed, a much loved and respected member of the Beached crew died, and we decided to hold a minutes silence as a tribute to him right before the main band were due to perform on the Saturday night. As M.C. it was down to me to get the rest of the Beached crew onto the stage and to ask the audience to remain quiet. Jim could see the tears in my eyes and offered to stand in. I appreciated the gesture but Ed had been a friend of mine as well and there was no way I was not going to do what had to be done. When the time came, everyone connected with Beached formed a line right across the front of the stage. I said something and the lighting guys projected Ed's image up onto the backcloth. We all turned to look at it and everyone fell silent for the full minute, including the audience. It was the most touching moment in the Beached history.

Mr Jim went on to run The Spa pub and then, in conjunction with Josh Woodhead, Indigo Alley which is really his spiritual home considering the history of the place. Somehow he managed to rekindle the musical vibe I enjoyed there back in the "Up For It Days". He is also the organiser of The Headland Festival held a few miles out of Scarborough and is the only man in my long and varied history to get me to sleep in a tent for three full nights. Recently he left running the pub to work for a Scarborough Arts association but still organises the pubs music.

Steve "Dicko" Dickinson is another friend from the Beached days. He, alongside Mel, his wife, runs the Scarborough cafe Mojo's, famous for good food and its Wednesday afternoon acoustic gigs. When Beached eventually finished he organised a series of all day acoustic gigs in Scarborough's Peasholm Park, called The "Acoustic Gathering" and that I acted as host. The stage was in the middle of the boating lake which made for getting the artists on and off both tricky and amusing. Yes I did fall in, just the once, but thank God it was at the side as we loaded the dragon boat and not in front of the audience. I had to introduce the remarkably brilliant Edwina Hayes whilst I was dripping wet with water sloshing out of my boots, a fact she's never forgotten.

Again there were many magical nights and memories, especially the one of Nick Harper playing Frank Zappa's song "Titties and Beer" as an encore for me as he floated in a rowing boat between the stage and the audience. Steve and I fell out for a couple of years due to a daft argument we had concerning stage lights. Eventually I realised that life is much too short for shit like that and we kissed and made up one night. He too became pissed off with the attitude of Scarborough Council who seemed object to the success of the "Acoustic Gathering" and like they did with "Beached", threw increased costs and problems at the gig. Eventually he stopped staging it and instead began to organise a Science Fiction convention at the Scarborough Spa, a place where the council have no say as they sold of their interest in the place to a private company. It's just had its fifth event and it's a brilliant event. Even if you don't like Sci-fi its worth seeing just for the cosplay enthusiasts. I take a stand there every year selling my Agnes the Scarborough Witch novels.

It amazes me that the council can be so myopic in killing off the goose (or geese) that lays the golden egg. Beached used to attract thousands to the town. I know because I used to stand on the stage and speak to them. Many of them stayed either one or two nights in the town, many of them spent money in the bars, in the fish and chip shops, in the ice cream shops, in the Harbour Bar, in the amusements and the town benefitted from the kudos of these visitors and the visiting bands. It put Scarborough on the map. It was the same with the Acoustic Gathering. That was held in a council owned park with a council owned cafe and council owned boating lake that always had a queue waiting to sail on the council owned dragon headed boats. How could they not make money?

I've lived in Scarborough now for twenty years and never in my life have I lived in a place where the council have seemed so intent on destroying the very thing that makes the town popular. Let's take the case of the Futurist Theatre. It was an amazing theatre on the seafront, on prime land. It dated back to beyond the last century, to the eighteen hundreds when it became a theatre and when film arrived doubled up as a cinema. It saw just about every star there has been since the 1900's. It saw the Beatles, each summer it was filled by excited holiday makers going to see Morecambe and Wise, or Ken Dodd. Then someone in the council saw an opportunity to make some money. I was standing in the Leeds Arms one night just after the 2004 Beached Festival when I was approached by a slightly tipsy member of Scarborough Council. a certain Tom Fox. He said he wanted my support and the support of all the Beached organisers. When I asked him why he simply replied -

"I want to pull the Futurist down!"

I laughed, it seemed such a ridiculous idea. Little did I know that Conservative councillors like to play the long game. It took ten years and despite public protests, despite a petition that Tom Fox himself refused to accept, despite it being against the will of the people he was meant to represent, the grand old theatre was flattened in 2018. Protests continued right up to the moment the bulldozers moved in. I performed my own take on the subject in a poem that I performed around the town at gigs and open mics until the last brick was squashed into the large, grey, uninspiring empty space that represents the legacy of Scarborough Conservatives.

The Futurist
Everybody knows
Our councils got no brains
Everybody knows
They can't even sort out drains

Everybody knows
They're not philanthropists
But what the fuck they're doing
Pulling down the Futurist

Flamingoland's paid thousands
Into Scarborough Tory coffers
Maybe to make sure
There are no other offers

Conservation, preservation
And heritage go west
Just so our local councillors
Can feather a secret nest.

We lost the Flora Gardens
The Opera House and more
Tourist information centres
Closed down for evermore
They're pulling down our town
And selling off the ground
It'll only cost 4 million quid
To knock the Futurist down

Cultural vandals in

The corridors of power
If the buggers were in Blackpool
They'd be selling off the Tower

No matter how loud we shout
The council still won't listen
Our opinions don't matter
They ignored the signed petition

Corruption in the council
That's not for me to say
But the message from the people is
We want the Futurist to stay!
Graham Rhodes

Feeling the need to express myself in a more artistic manner I suddenly discovered photography. In my life I'd been a graphic designer, a/v designer, video director and video producer, all visual arts. Now after picking up a camera and taking photographs I played with the images on a computer. Suddenly I was creating images that were interesting. More than interesting, they could be saleable. I shopped around and in March 2009 I managed to get myself a small one man exhibition at Sewerby Hall, a semi-stately home near Bridlington. It was well received and I took a stall at a open air event on Scarborough's West Pier called Seafest. I sold a lot of pictures. Whilst I was there I looked at the building on the pier. Up on a balcony there were a series of small offices, one of them was up for rent. I contacted the council and after some deliberation I was allowed to open one up as a small gallery. In 2009 Aakschipper Images Gallery was born.

Now I was a gallery owner, and still writing scripts I didn't have a lot of spare time and I left the theatre company that unfortunately folded shortly after.

Then, out of the blue in 2013, I was asked to perform a set of my poetry at a fringe event at the Scarborough Literary Festival. It was to be held in Woodend, the old museum that had become an arts hub. That is they rented rooms out to artists and companies with an arts focus, as well as a gallery and a performance space. I'd been there before. I'd attended a couple of openings and meetings and such but it was all a bit corporate for me. I preferred my little gallery down on the pier. I mean if you can sell art above a public toilet and two doors down from a fish market, well you can sell art anywhere. It's just that it didn't or doesn't sell as much as it needs to. There again it hasn't lost me a lot of money!

Anyway I accepted the gig at Woodend and I made it into the official programme. This is what they said of me –

"Graham Rhodes: Rock and Roll Poet "Out of Retirement" for One Night Only...."
Sat 13th April 2013 7-8pm
Woodend Creative Space

Graham Rhodes began reading poetry in Leeds Folk clubs back in the 1960's. For over forty years he has performed his poetry in raucous rock n roll venues throughout the North and Scotland. This is Graham's first poetry gig since 2006 and we have him for one night only...."

I pulled in a couple of favours from a production company I wrote scripts for and a video crew from Leeds came along and videoed the entire gig. You can see the results today on You Tube.

An hour seems a long time until you actually get up there and the time simply flashes past. I think I managed to overrun. For weeks before I stressed myself as to what I was going to read. Then a week before the gig I had an idea. I decided to play poetry roulette. That is I spread all my poetry out face down, like a magician spreads out a pack of cards and asked members of the audience to choose a poem. That way there was no theme and it was all random. Before I read the selected poem out I explained the time and reason why I wrote it. It seemed to go very well, each poem got applauded and at the end I got a good reception. It whetted my appetite for live readings again.

I kept up my friendship with Jerry Scott and when he left BBC Radio York he set up a radio station in Woodend. Unsurprisingly he called it Radio Scarborough, and after broadcasting for a while he asked me if I'd like to create and present a late night programme, and so Rommelpot was born. The rationale behind the program is that I only play music that hasn't been a hit, in fact in some cases hasn't been listened to at all. It's by artists that not only dropped off the radar but probably never got on it in the first place. Old 1950's rockabilly, late 50's rock and roll, 1960's pop and psychedelic bands , 1970's psychobilly, punk, new wave, right up to new stuff that never gets air play today. Along the way I play stuff by old acquaintances like Beau, and Tony Capstick alongside the likes of Wally and Toby Jepson. Oddly enough, for a spoken word performer I never say much on air. When it comes to playing records I belong to the John Peel DJ school. I say little but play as much music as possible. I've never believed in the DJ as a star, I've always believed that they are there to play music and nothing else. Anyway the program has been going now nearly every week for five years, it even has a Facebook page where you can catch up with old broadcasts on Mixcloud.

My relationship of 14 years blew apart in 2015 when my wife and I split up which, as it turned out she was having an affair, proved both hurtful and difficult as we had married back in 2008 and jointly bought a house together in Scarborough's Old Town. It took five years and a £3,000 solicitors bill to disentangle myself from that relationship. Here's a bit of advice. Never believe anyone who tells you –

"Let's make it an agreeable separation. We'll go to mediation and get things sorted and agreed between us. it won't cost too much!"

Huh so much for that theory. We did go to mediation. We did get things sorted, or so I thought. Then we took it to a solicitor for final agreement signatures. He agreed to a basic fixed fee of £365.00. Then her letters started flying. Every time my solicitor sent a letter with the final offer she found some other little point to complain about. This exchange of letters went on from February to the following November, most of 2018. By that time she agreed to every little dotted "i" and every little crossed "t" the solicitor had run out of patience and the £365 fixed fee turned out to be a bill that reflected the amount of work she had singlehandedly caused. It came to £3,000! Even worse she blamed me for it and I was left to pay the bill. So much for agreeing things in advance.

The separation left me reeling. I didn't know what to do. Then I bumped into a singer songwriter I knew called Jesse Hutchinson. Actually it's not accurate to just call him that, Jesse is a lot more than a singer, he's a rather special guitar virtuoso and a great singer. He realised I was down and told me to try my poetry again. He had a Thursday night residency at a Scarborough pub called The Cellars and asked me to fill in for his beer break. I did, and continued doing it almost every Thursday night, right through from October to the following Christmas. I soon got tired of reading the old stuff and began writing again. A couple of years ago I returned to the venue perform a special poem as Jesse was celebrating his 500th gig at the small Scarborough Bar, (as well as a great Wednesday open mic it also does rather wonderful Sunday lunches!) This is the poem I wrote for Jesse.

Five Hundred Gigs

Five Hundred gigs
All in the same place
Some sort of weird continuum
In both time and space
Everyone is happy with a smile
upon their face
just don't dare to sit
in someone else's place.

Five hundred gigs
Just in Cellars bar
People flock from miles around
By taxi, bus and car
From Bridlington and Whitby
And places so afar
Just to see young Jesse
Play his old guitar

Five hundred gigs
Five thousand broken strings.
A hundred thousand songs
Our Jesses had to sing
Americana, Texacana
Country and western swing
He's even covered Donovan
And that Sunshine Superman thing

Five Hundred gigs
For a treetop flyer

Five hundred gigs
And the bar gets higher
On Monkey Wrench
And Farmers too
Neil Young covers
Just for me and you

Graceland and St Judy's Comet
Boots of Spanish Leather
Winding Wheels and Oxford Town
Fifty Ways to Leave Your Lover
Hearts and Bones, Ophelia
My Sweet Carolina
Crosby Stills and Hutchinson
Nothing could be finer

So thank you My Hutchinson
From a grateful Cellars crew
Happy Five Hundredth birthday
From all of us here, to you.
Graham Rhodes

I was pleased to be asked to repeat the poem his 2019 gig to celebrate the release of Jesse's CD "No Direction Home."

Since I've known him Jesse has been in and out of a number of bands. One of which has now morphed into The Rough Cut's and features a singer from Robin Hoods Bay called Luke Pearson who in my opinion is one of the UK's best white soul singers. He reminds me of the 60's greats Long John Baldry and Chris Farlow. Now the reason I mention this is that I supported them at the Grosvenor at Robin Hoods Bay and that night was special because it was the first time I performed a new anti fracking poem. The performance was captured on video and can be seen on You Tube.

For many years a lot of my poetry has been political. I've taunted, lampooned and insulted the Conservative party as long as I've been writing. In fact looking at my work, over the years I've written more stuff under the Tories than I have under Labour. Take from that what you will. Today, post coalition, post Theresa May with characters like Michael Gove, Boris Johnson and Jacob Rees Mogg in positions of power my pen has never been busier. However one thing that scares me, and should scare you too, is fracking. I fear the ramifications of squirting high pressure chemical filled water deep underground. I have a friend called Stuart Ackroyd who actually spends time protesting at fracking sites and on the HS2 route. To me he's a bit of a hero, whenever I perform this poem I always dedicate it to him. However, as I write this, the news has just broken that the Government has stopped all fracking operations throughout England. Let's see if they hold onto that promise. I like to think the following poem had something to do with this decision. It' didn't, but I like to think it did!

Anti-Fracking Poem

Fuckity Fuckity Fuckity Fuck
Sold out by the council
To make a quick buck
Fuckity Fuckity Fuckity Fuck
The North Yorkshire Councillors
Really do suck!

Frackity Frackity Frackity Frack
Once you've ruined the water
You can't put it back

Yorkshire Conservatives
Took Third Energies shilling

*Selling out all the people
Who are against all the drilling
Poison the aquifer, poison the land
All for the sake of a few hundred grand*

*Bugger the farmers the sheep and the ewes
Bugger the tourist whose here for the views
Conservative councillors in the Government's pay
They'll end up with knighthoods for the votes cast today
Dancing like puppets to Cameron's jigs
Now he's screwed everyone one of use
and not just dead pigs.*

*Sod conservation and all public wishes
flames up your plug hole when you're doing the dishes
when everything falls down a bloody great crack
They'll be sorry they gave permission to frack*

*Frackity Frackit Frackitty Frack
Once you've extracted the shale gas
You can't put it back*

*Frackety Frackity Frackity Frick
It's not just the water that's making us sick*

*Who'll explain to the children
Why the fish are all dead
Who'll explain to the drinkers
Why the waters all red
Who'll explain to the tourists
Who'll all turn away
Why North Yorkshire council
Voted that way*

Westminster coffers fill up with gold
Buts it's our children's birthright they just bought and sold
Frackity Frackity Frackity Frack
Once you've ruined the country you can't put it back!
Graham Rhodes

It was good to be writing again. I got involved with a bloke called Richard who was trying to get a magazine started and had involved Captain Ants, so I joined in with him. I must have written around twenty or so articles but somehow, I don't think the magazine made it past issue three. It was after hanging around with him a couple of months that I began to realise he wasn't quite what he claimed. I mean, did he really expect me to believe he was the booking agent for BBC's Pebble Mill. That he stepped in for John Bonham and saved a Led Zepplin recording session! That he was Kirsty McColl's lover? Oh come on. He blagged a joint radio program with me on Radio Scarborough and before anyone knew what had happened he'd wormed his way into the position of Station Manager. Needless to say there was a lot of politics and eventually Jerry, who had now been diagnosed with cancer left to form another radio station.

The birth of Coast and County Radio occurred 2016 and after a while I joined it along with my Rommelpot show. Unfortunately Jerry lost his battle with the disease at the end of that year. His ashes were put into a rocket that was fired over Scarborough's South Bay at the following years Scarborough Sci-Fi Convention. It went with a mighty whoosh, and sent a cascade of stars over the moonlit sea, watched by his friends and the people from the convention that he had always played a large part in, it was a spectacular way to go. He is much missed.

I left Radio Scarborough by telling Richard and the two other directors exactly what I thought of them. I then suffered the most damming thing that can happen in this day and age. I was unfriended on Facebook. That night I lay in bed fuming and in one brief, ten minute rant, wrote what was to become one of my most popular poems ever. It's dedicated to Richard and so far I have had the pleasure of performing the poem four or five times when he has been in the audience. To this day I'm not sure whether he knows he's the reason behind it. I have performed it so many times at The Merchant open mic that when I do it the other performers join in. It's almost become a communal poem.

Facebook Poem
I've just been un-friended on Facebook
Does it look like that I give a shit
Thank God that you'll no longer share with me
Your thoughts and your wisdom and wit

No longer will I have to put up with
You opinions and photos of life
Your comical cats and photos of twats
That you meet when you're out with your wife

I've just been un-friended on Facebook
Hip- hip- hip bloody hurray
No more dubious comments on Brexit
And your fetish about Theresa May

No more misguided missives from fascists
Jokes that are sexist and fail
Your comments on everyday living
Taken from t' Telegraph, Sun and The Mail

I've just been un-friended on Facebook

Now I'm liberated, cleansed and feel free
From all of your dubious comments
Why the fuck did you send them to me?

Now you can carry on living
You're day to day life in your way
And I'll get on doing whatever I do
Not caring what your Facebook might say.

I've just been un-friended on Facebook
I assume that you now wish-me ill luck
But I'm sorry to say I've have a great day
And frankly I don't give a fuck.

Graham Rhodes

The Christmas after my marriage split up I went to the Stephen Joseph Theatre to see an old friend called Anna Shannon perform one of her rare Scarborough gigs. Afterwards I got talking to her and a lady called Cheryl Govan, Director of Young People and Community at the SJT. I have no idea what we talked about. I only know that something clicked and that night I went home and picked up a pen and began to write a novel.

Over the years I've tried to write many novels and always failed most miserably so I didn't hold any great hopes. This one began a bit shaky but as it went on it gained a power and a momentum. I had never come across anything like this before. Before long the damn thing was writing itself. After four weeks I sat back. I had written a novel. It was called "A Witch, her Cat and a Pirate." It was a historical fantasy based around Agnes, a three hundred year old witch that lived in present day Scarborough Old Town with an old beaten up cat called Marmaduke. When the pair of them go down her cellar and go through a door that isn't there, they come out in 18th century Scarborough and Marmaduke turns into a six foot high, one eared, one eyed, ex-highwayman and her right hand man through all her adventures.

The storyline was based on the true story of the Battle of Flamborough, the only battle in the American War of Independence that didn't happen in America. I can see the site looking out of my gallery window. In the encounter a sea captain called John Paul Jones attempted to capture the Baltic Fleet and went into battle with the British Navy and won. Ironically the losing British sea captain was called Richard Pearson! The history I wrote about was accurate as some years previously, back in the mid nineties, I had written a script about John Paul Jones and an agent even got it across to America. It came back quicker that it went but at least there was a little interest. Now that research came into play as I wrote about the lead up to the battle with a more "fantastic" story. I was pleased with the result, but before I could sit back and reflect on what I had done I discovered I missed writing, and I missed Agnes and Marmaduke and before I realised it I began to write a second, then a third and a fourth.

Agnes completely took me over. I always wrote her stories at night, in a series of large £3 lined notebooks and "Soft touch rollerball pens" £1 for 3, both purchased from The Works. Today I have a large pile of these notebooks at the side of my bed in the hope that one day they might be worth something.

I did try to get them published and sent the first three chapters and a synopsis (like they all ask for) to every agent and publishing company I could find on Google. What a complete and utter waste of time and resources that proved to be. Both publishers and agents, when any of them could be bothered answering, were slick and glib and patronising and offered all the usual excuses for not wanting to handle the work. I got the lot from "It's not our genre" to "We're not looking for this sort of material at the moment." I was amazed. Not one encouraging or constructive answer came from any of them.

I also discovered an amazing fact. There's not one literary agency in the North of England, at least not one that I could find. They all seem to be in London and blest with that special London snobbery that subscribes to the belief that no creative work is ever done north of the M25. If by any chance I sound bitter it's because I am. Agnes stayed in my computer.

When I got together with a Leeds lady called Yvonne I mentioned that these books were in the memory banks of my computer. She laughed and asked me what they were doing there and why weren't they published. I told her about agents. She told me to do it myself. So I did. It wasn't cheap and I've maxed out a credit card in buying stock, but up to present I have published nine of the Agnes novels, thanks to Amazon where they are now on sale as both paperbacks and Kindle versions. I also sell them in my gallery.

I have also republished my York book "Footprints in the Mud of Time." and published "The Jazz Detective", a detective novel set in London in the 1950's Soho that I wrote back in the 1990's, forgot about and finished it off between writing the Agnes novels.

I then published my book of poetry, "The Collected Poems 72-16" and a Sci-Fi Novel called "Orcas Teeth." Yes I know, Amazon screw us all over on their non-payment of taxes, and I'm not defending them but, as what they are doing is perfectly legal, isn't it up to the Government to stop the legal tax loopholes? Personally I'm grateful to Amazon for giving us "want-to-be-authors" an opportunity to get our work in front of the public, who after all are the biggest arbitrators of taste.

To date Agnes has confounded Dutch spies, fought Vikings and Devil Dogs, met a Finnish death metal band, helped destroy an out-of-time submarine, met George Washington, and had a sort of "Pirates of The Caribbean" type adventure. There are another two finished, just waiting to be typed out. I have had the most amazing head fun writing her adventures, and I'm constantly amazed to meet her readers who seem to love her and follow all her adventures. In fact some of them I've met know more about her than I do, especially one lady who proclaimed that she had found Agnes's grave which, as she is a fictional character, must have taken some doing.

I suppose here's a good place to explain why I write. At first I felt I just had to do something to get onto that stage, to be a performer, then I began to realise the I had something to say, hence the poetry.

Then I became a scriptwriter and discovered that scriptwriting isn't difficult because it is always dialogue. With scripts, especially the corporate, or marketing, or training scripts I write, you only have to worry about the facts and the style of the dialogue. You don't have to paint a portrait of the characters or create heavily descriptive background scenes like you do in a short story or book. A script is basically a skeleton on which other people hang the flesh. Plus a script is something I get paid for. With scriptwriting it's no use being arty and waiting for that illusive muse. A script is the first part of a production process, either for a video or a conference. Both of them have deadlines; both of them have other people down the line waiting to start their part of the process. You can't blow a deadline when you're writing corporate scripts for production companies. If you do you simply don't work again.

That really sharpens you up and kills the myth of waiting for a muse, or waiting until you feel creative. The inspiration for scriptwriting is and always has been looking forward to the cheque at the end of the process. If that sounds mercenary well, perhaps it is, but it's also necessary to keep a roof over your head.

A book is different, a book needs to have descriptions of the characters, descriptions of the locations and scenes, a book is creating in words the whole damn picture including the colours, the light and the shade. It is a completely different way of writing. The other thing about novel writing is that, apart from the fact there's no money at the end of the process, it's a bloody lonely occupation. I do most of my writing at night, sometimes from 7.15 after The Archers and if I'm on a roll, continue to write until three or four the following morning, with either Radio 4 or Radio 5 Live droning on in the background. 5 Live if its Monday and the football season. I always write in bed. That way when you are tired or fall asleep you're already in the right place, the down side is that all my sheets and duvet covers have ink stains on them!

Why Agnes and why a witch? I really have no idea. The basic idea came to me and I simply wrote it. They say always write about something you know. Well I based the book in Scarborough, in the house where I actually lived, so I know the surrounding area and streets, and they haven't changed much in the last three hundred years. I knew about John Paul Jones and his story so I was able to theorise about him and his mission against Great Britain. I knew nothing about witches, but I have a brain and as I've written many historical scripts, I know how to do accurate research. That's really all I needed.

Looking back I really do believe that the books wrote themselves. I can remember in book two "A Witch Her Cat and the

Ship Wreckers", a character rode by and originally he was meant to be someone who was simply to give Marmaduke some directions and ride on. Instead he burst into the book, became a main character and Dancing Jack was born. Seconds before writing and naming him I had no idea he existed. Now he's a main character in at least three or four of the books. I simply can't explain it. It's been the same in all the Agnes books I've written. Characters come and go by themselves without me really inviting them in. They're not major best sellers but they do sell. I sell them from my gallery, and a shop in the centre of Scarborough sells them, and like I say, they are available via Amazon. Agnes has her own Facebook page, a web site and a fan base that is slowly building up. I've also made a surprising discovery. When I began writing the books I had no idea of who I was writing for. At the back of my head I suppose it was the teenage Harry Potter audience. It turns out that my audience is women. Over eighty percent of my readers are woman aged from thirty upwards. Somehow I think I've created a feminist icon.

In an attempt to attract tourists Scarborough has created a number of festivals. Coastival is an Arts festival that occurs in February on a yearly basis and in 2017 I staged a gig under its Coastival banner. It was called Wordsmiths and I held it in the Cellars Bar on Sunday Feb 19th, the last day of the festival. On the bill were Scarborough singer songwriters Frankie Dixon, Alistair James and Ross Dransfield and spoken word artists Dave Pruckner, (yes that Dave Pruckner) James Koppert and myself. It seemed to go well. Dave was as witty and funny as always, (we worked out we've now been performing together for fifty years), whilst James is actually a hip hop artist his performances are always powerful and heartfelt, he is well worth checking out.

Alistair James is probably one of the best musicians around. His voice is amazing, his choice of material vast and he plays guitar and drums equally brilliantly. One of the great pleasures in my life had been watching his performances grow in stature over the years.

Ross Dransfield is also an excellent singer song writer and hosts the open mic night at The Merchant pub where I seem to have residency.

Frankie Dixon also deserves a word here. She is the ex-girlfriend of Jesse Hutchinson and is an amazing singer songwriter in her own right. When they spilt up she was left with a gap for a series of three gigs she had arranged at Woodend Creative Space, and she asked me to step in. They were three gigs I really enjoyed. For a start they were in a concert style and not in a noisy pub and I was able to perform a number of poems I don't normally do. Plus at one of the gigs I actually sat down and read excerpts from my book "A View from Inside the Pink Monster" and "Footprints in the Mud of Time." You can see some of these performances on You Tube. I really enjoyed doing them. I quiet like being treated as an author. I've done a similar reading at a small sea front cafe called The Seastrand. I always find it both challenging and interesting when an audience asks me questions about writing and the characters that I write about.

I never seem to perform them these days but I love monologues like the ones Bob Williamson introduced me to all those years ago. I also like writing daft little rhymes. Here's an example of both –

Boudicca and the Romans
The Romans had landed in Briton
And building aqueducts, villas and roads
They were doing quite well with the conquering

the poor Britain's who only wore woad.

Then they came to the boundaries of Yorkshire
Where the Icini ruled as top tribe
They were led by a Queen called Boudicca
That the Romans thought they could bribe

So they sent her some wine in amphorae
Roast dormice in sesame seeds
But the Icini were brought up on black pudding
Served with tatties and turnips and mead

They looked at the Roman food parcel
And poked it with swords and with spears
Then Boudicca stood tall, and said to them all
You're not building roads around here

Now the Romans were working to contract
And were already late in their deeds
They'd got lost in a bog down in Thetford
And fell in the river in Leeds

Building roads in straight lines proved a problem
In a country full of grey clouds and mist
Where no one could see the horizon
And it were proving a bit hit and miss

So they sat down and came to agreement
To save bloodshed and more double pay
T'Romans stopped at Boudicca's boundary
Waved their Eagles, then just walked away.

And that why if you go into Yorkshire
The roads are all bent, twisted and poor

And why it takes hours to travel
The length of the A64.
Graham Rhodes

Nude Telly
There's nude dating on the telly
Willies in HD 3D
They scared the cat last evening
And put me off my tea.
Graham Rhodes

    To perform these types of poems I need a seated, listening audience. Performing in the places I usually do I always get the noisy loud lot that you have to shout and go through a couple of shock tactics before you can get them to listen. I've started my set with this poem for the last five years now. It generally get's the audience's attention and shuts them up.

This Poem Is Shit
You can be shit faced
Have shit for brains
Shit or get off the pot

Smoke shit
Talk shit
Or just be shit hot

You can throw shit
Give a shit
Or duck when it hits the fan

You can be in deep shit

Tough shit
When everything turns wrong

You can look like shit
Feel shit
Go like shit off a shovel

Find yourself
up shit creek
without any paddle

Have a shower of shit
Get your shit together
Bears shit in the woos cos its always shitty weather

There's heavy shit
Weird shit
But please don't be offended
This is just a shitty poem
I'm just fucking glad its ended.
Graham Rhodes

Since I've got back in front of a microphone I have gigged constantly, mainly at the Scarborough open mics held at The Merchant, thank you Ross Dransfield, and at The Cellars, thank you John Watton. I have also done open mics and supported bands at Indigo Ally and for me, where my Scarborough adventure began twenty years ago, it's a bit like coming home.

The years 2017 and 2018 were incredible for the amount of young musicians that came out of a Scarborough college, mainly due to a great teacher and founder of the band Danse Society, Paolo Aiello. Most of them have now moved on to universities across the country, but for a couple of years, alongside the older more established Scarborough musicians they made the pubs and the town swing. All of them.

One of the bands that formed from that college is called Northern Riots and I'm lucky that they like what I do and asked me to open up their gigs for them. Thanks to them I've appeared in a number of York rock pubs, and rediscovered Leeds in the shape of The Primrose pub. They are a dynamic young band with hopefully, a great future ahead of them. (You met them in the introduction)

In 2018 Ross staged a few gigs in Scarborough Market. One of them featured Ross Dransfield, Jesses Hutchinson, myself and Dave Pruckner. Yes Dave and I are still together after all these years, or to quote the late Bob Williamson "still hazy after all these beers!"

Speaking of which in 2018 I staged three gigs on three successive nights in Indigo Ally under the banner, and in aid of "We Shall Overcome!" Let me explain that.

The day after Theresa May won her election, albeit with a reduced majority, Joe Solo breezed into my gallery. We've got to do something about austerity, he said. I suggested holding a gig. The next time I saw him would be about two or three months later. I asked how the gig idea was going. He explained that so far he had around seventy planned up and down the country. You see Joe is a very popular left wing singer songwriter and all he did was float the idea of a gig where the admittance money was food for food banks, clothing, and later on sanitary products, all of which go to the local food banks. People liked the idea and it grew. At the last count its estimated there have been 750 gigs in 142 towns across 9 countries on 3 continents, raising an estimated £350,000 of cash, food, clothing and bedding for those at the sharp end of austerity.

Personally I'm bloody proud to have played a very small part in its inception. Anyway just after my 69th birthday I managed to put a bill together that filled Indigo Ally for three consecutive nights. I called on favours from many musicians and bands that I now call friends. The headliners on the three nights were Northern Riots, The Fuzz Junkies and The Feens and, thanks to Indigo Alley donating a percentage of the bar takings, we managed to raise a decent amount of clothing, food and money that was donated to Scarborough's Rainbow Centre.

As I've already said, Joe Solo is a very good and prolific songwriter, mainly writing political songs. He sings at political rallies and at political gatherings. In 2018 he invited me to MC and read my poems at the May Day Festival of Solidarity in Barnsley. It was the first time I had been back to the town since my one-man show of pit drawing all those years ago. I enjoyed the occasion which was made even better by introducing a singer called Reg Meuross who wrote one of my all time favourite songs "My Name Is London Town." It's lyrics take me right back to my time there. It even mentions St Catherine's Dock, the place where I went for a drink to sort out the British Airways "Route 66" problem. It was a privilege and a pleasure introducing him and sitting listening to him play the song.

One of Joe Solos songs isn't political and he never performs it. In my opinion it's one of the best song he has ever written. It's called "Ghosts and Drunks" and he passed it onto a friend of his who recorded it. Sometime check out "Ghosts and Drunks" by Boss Caine. It's on a compilation CD called "Best of York", which gives us a clue that Boss Caine hails from York. He has an amazing voice and after hearing his version of Joes song I had to listen to more of his material. He's a bit difficult to categorise, probably alt country if you want a label. Vocally he reminds me of early Tom Waits around the time of his album "Closing Time." I mentioned this to Joe who informed me that Boss Caine, real name Daniel Lucas, ran an open mic in York called "Busk at Dusk". It was upstairs in the Dusk Bar and began around 10.30 on a Sunday night and ran until 2.00am. I mentioned this to Yvonne and as I had a birthday coming up we decided to treat ourselves to a night away. We booked ourselves a room in an hotel and, via Facebook, I arranged with Daniel to do a spot.

At the gig I introduced myself to Daniel and sat and watched the acts. He began the night, and as he knew I loved the Joe Solo song, and he knew it was my birthday, he played it. Trust me it's even better live. When it came to my turn, just as I walked onto the performance area, he looked at me and came up close.

"Let's see what you can do!" He whispered.

I love a challenge and began with my usual opening poem. Three poems into my set his head appeared around a corner. He smiled and gave me a broad wink. Since then I've been back once more. For Yvonne that particular night will always be memorable for me trying to check us into the wrong hotel, twice!. The one I'd booked wasn't where I thought it was!

Later that year I also did a "We Shall Overcome" gig with Boss Caine where he previewed his new album "Loved by Trouble, Troubled By Love". It was staged at Fibbers at its new location on York's Toft Green. Despite its move the place still had the same vibe as the old Fibbers at Stonebow, and the dressing room was still a shambles, but the fridge was nicely stocked.

In November 2018 myself and Yvonne had an evening in Leeds with Dave Pruckner and his wife. I told him of my recent cancer scare and the tests I had undergone and the fact that my ex had landed me with a huge solicitors bill. The following morning I found this poem on my Facebook feed. It brilliantly summed up my previous two weeks.

A £3,000 Solicitor's Bill and an Air-Pump up the Arse

I was hoping for a clean break and a clean bill of health
But between the solicitor and the hospital is where I found myself
My ex-wife is trying to bleed me dry and my doctor says my health's not good
The legal costs are piling up and now I find I'm losing blood
Times are tough and laughs are sparse
When you've got a £3,000 solicitor's bill

and an air-pump up the arse

I'd hoped we'd separate amicably with civility and no raised voices
I'd hoped I'd always have my health despite some dodgy lifestyle choices
But two things that are guaranteed to leave you with mental scars
Are a £3,000 solicitor's bill and an air-pump up the arse

Now medical examinations are rarely fun
And messy divorce proceedings don't cheer anyone
But believe me, it feels like it's the final cut
When you've got a hole in your wallet and a pain in your butt
But you try to keep on smiling, thinking it could be worse
Then you get a £3,000 solicitor's bill and an air-pump up the arse

These things are sent to try us, that's what my mother used to say
But when you've had the full medical spectrum
And an air-pipe up your rectum
It's hard not to feel some dismay

And when a lawyer's filled you full of dread
And a surgeon's filled you full of gas
You're left with a £3,000 solicitor's bill and an air-pump up the arse

Now I'm not one for complaining, I start each day hoping for the best
But when your ex-spouse wants the house from under you
And the consultant wants to run more tests
When your life's turned upside down and it's bordering on farce
Here comes a £3,000 solicitor's bill and an air-pump up the arse.

Dave Pruckner

Ironically in the early hours of the following morning I woke up with a pain in my chest and the paramedics were called and I was taken to Leeds famous St, James Infirmary who after five or six hours, diagnosed me with trapped wind. I travelled back to Scarborough on the train but on the Tuesday morning woke up in so much pain that my lodger, Julia Wray, the brilliant saxophone player, eventually demanded I went to the doctor. Being unable to move I rang the owner of Coast and County Radio, Dave McGregor who kindly dropped everything and drove me to the surgery where the doctor took one look at me, wrote a note and told Dave he was to take me to A&E straight away, there wasn't time for an ambulance. Inside the hour I was tucked up in bed inside the cardiac unit with tubes and wires taped to my body.

Again I survived. After a series of tests it was discovered that an artery had collapsed in my heart and, after being shipped to a second hospital to have a stent inserted, I was discharged back into the care of Dave McGregor who kindly drove me back home. The whole process took ten days, during which Julia kindly looked after my cats. That Christmas Yvonne spent with me in

Scarborough and I underwent three months convalescence lying on the sofa binging on gin and Netflix. Gin because once again I had to give up smoking. That was where the idea for this book was dreamt up. Well, when you look your own mortality right in the eye and you realise you have a tale to tell and haven't told it, then it's time to do something about it.

So whose this book for? I have no idea. I suppose it's for the people who, over the years have seen me perform and enjoyed my work. However I really hope its picked up by someone young, someone who can't play an instrument, but likes writing words. I hope it gives them hope and inspires them in their own way to find their voice. If that's you just remember, this is not a manual – it's just my story.

I have always defended the National Health. They have saved my life at least three, maybe four times. I have always found them to be staffed by wonderful people who care, no matter what state you are in. Twice now I've experienced the expertise and care offered by the Scarborough General Hospital Cardiac Unit. Back in the day I watched my daughter being born in St Thomas's Hospital in London. York hospital helped to diagnose and cure me when I was diagnosed with ITP, and patched me up after I accidently fell from the top of a factory roof. As long as I have breath in my body I will always support and defend the principle of free care at the point of delivery along with supporting the many brilliant, caring people who provide that service. Hence these two poems that are still, and always will be, in my act -

Virgin on the ridiculous
It's all gone bloody silly
Bordering on daft
What do you think you are doing?
You having a fucking laugh?

You're beginning to take the piss mate
You're pulling on my leg
You're pulling on my plonker
You're messing up my head
You've started taking liberties
You're getting on my wick
We used to have respect for you
But now you're acting like a prick
You've spoilt your reputation
You've gone and marked your card
You're off your bloody rocker mate
You're out your tiny mind
You're living in a fantasy
Stuck in your own dream
Your attitudes and platitudes
Just make me want to scream
How come they think you're qualified
To make trains all run on time
You've dropped a mighty bollock
On that Virgin, East Coast Mainline
So come on Richard Branson
With your hidden, off- shore wealth
Show you care, sell off your shares
And stop buying-up our National Health
Graham Rhodes

Happiness
Happiness comes with
A Whisper Bar
Or a knickerbocker glory
in the Harbour Bar

an unexpected orgasm
or a tax rebate
paying off your debts
wiping clean the slate

Happiness comes
with a new CD
discovering you haven't got
an STD

finding a tenner
in an old jacket pocket
lighting up a joint
that takes off like a rocket

happiness comes
with a living wage
food in your stomach
and a pension in old age

a society that cares
for its ill and sick
and not been sold
to money grabbing pricks

who starve it of cash
to make sure it fails
so say it loud - say it proud
 National Health is not for sale.
Graham Rhodes

Just in case you have no idea what the "Harbour Bar" reference is in the above poem, it's the wonderful ice cream emporium on the Scarborough sea front, across the road from my gallery. Great ice cream, Horlicks, and rum flavoured coffee in winter, all served up inside a unique 1950's decor.

Scarborough is also blessed with the remarkable Fuzz Junkies, a trio that play originals and cover versions and do a version of Lynard Skynard's "Freebird" that rivals the original. I've spent many happy hours watching them play. The three of them are remarkable young musicians, I defy anyone to name me a better bass player than Elliot Pelucci, or a better guitarist than Stefan Ward and holding it all together with some great drumming there's Ryan Holland. One of the first gigs I went to after my heart attack was a Fuzz Junkies gig. I was amazed when Stefan surprised me by announcing that he had turned one of my poems "Nightsurfing" into a powerful almost metal song. It was brilliant, I absolutely loved that. Thanks guys.

Another singer I love is a tall, young man called Danny Firth. Somehow he has managed to incorporate my poem "Excitable Sadie" into a rap song. The first time I heard it I nearly fell off my seat. It's brilliant and when he performs it at the Merchant, where all the regulars know the poem, they all join in. Long may he continue with it. Thanks Danny, it's bloody brilliant.

I did my own first, post-heart attack gig, at the end of February 2019 supporting the Northern Riots at the Primrose Pub in Leeds. Getting back on stage was a scary thought and Yvonne, Dave and his wife Jackie came to lend moral support. The Primrose is an excellent place. It's a typical old Leeds pub that doesn't seem to have changed since the 1960's. It's the home of a great Leeds band called Steve Wood and the Hoods. The performance area is a large stage about six inches higher than the rest of the standing audience in an open room, painted black. When the stage lights are off the only light is from a large slit in the wall where the bar is. That night there were three bands on with Northern Riots topping the bill. I was due on stage directly before them. It was what I call a three whisky gig, that means I needed three whisky's before going on stage. As I mounted the stage I took a deep breath, grabbed the mic and began the familiar opening rant ...

"You can be shit faced,
Have shit for brains,
Shit or get off the pot..."

I did seven poems, end to end, without a break and came off stage to a huge round of applause. As Northern Riots kicked into their first song I went back into the bar and sat down. Someone had pinched my whisky! I was back and nothing had changed.

Since the heart attack I have continued making regular appearances at open mics at The Cellars and The Merchant, and started appearing in Leeds, mainly at The Crooners open mic. I have done a festival in Bradford and supported such bands as Eli & The Blues Prophets, Ronnie Wray's Blues Band, The Fuzz Junkies, Jesse Hutchinson, and the Northern Riots of course. I have even joined in with Captain Ants and his band "The Jawline of Julianne Moore." where I performed "Space Invaders", the first time it's been performed since the old Arkwright's Ferret days. I also performed my act at a charity gig in Scarborough's Cask pub supporting the one and only Grace Petrie where I swapped a copy of this book for two of her CD's.

As to the future, well I have a plan to leave Scarborough and to re-establish myself back in Leeds where I can get backwards and forwards to do gigs in Bradford, York and Leeds, without stopping in a hotel or an Airbnb. God knows, I'll miss Scarborough, the sea, my little gallery, the brilliant musical scene and the many brilliant friends I have made here in the last eighteen years, but even at 70 years old, my life holds further challenges and ambitions. That will be the next chapter, let's see how it works out.

The Next Chapter
2022 (Update)

    I finished the writing of this book back in 2019 when I was considering moving to Leeds. I didn't. I'd got as far as looking at property and doing the sums and could just afford a house somewhere in Armley, or in a low price area. I needed to move as the ex-wife was pressurising me with a blitz of solicitors letters to sell the jointly owned Scarborough house in Princess Street. I didn't want to sell, I liked it there but I knew the sale was inevitable, hence the house search. This search was still going on when on a dark and dismal Friday afternoon I travelled to Leeds. It was pouring down as I crossed Boar Lane and I trod on a piece of paper that was travelling along the gutter at a rate of knots. The next thing I knew was that I was laying on my back on the wet pavement. I couldn't move. I looked down and my foot was pointing in the wrong direction. It was obvious to me that something serious had happened. A couple of blokes ran up to me and asked if I was OK. No I wasn't.

    Carefully they lifted me up. The pain was indescribable. Looking around they found some scaffolding that surrounded a nearby building and by hanging my arms over the bottom row hung me from it. That was a great idea as I could lift my damaged leg off the floor and allow it to hang there. They rang for an ambulance only to be told there was a three hour wait. We all knew that waiting for that length of time wasn't an option. It was taking all my time and effort not to scream such was the pain. Eventually they decided to flag down a taxi. The fifth one we stopped agreed to take me to the Leeds General Infirmary, better known as the L.G.I.

Somehow the two men and driver managed to get me into the passenger seat where I curled up in a sort of foetal position and the driver set off at a steady pace. Yvonne was waiting for me at the entrance to the hospital and watched as two paramedics lifted me carefully out of the taxi, laid me on a stretcher and rushed me into A&E where I was given a series of pain killing drugs before being sent off to be x-rayed and examined.

To this day I will be grateful to the two guys who helped and stayed with me whilst they flagged the cab down. I was in so much pain that I never took their names or numbers and hence I never really thanked them for their kindness. The same with the cab driver. I am also grateful to Yvonne for staying with me as the medical processes took place and I was put into a bed in the ward.

My worst fears came true. I had broken my hip. In fact due to the fall I had managed to break the ball end of my bone and shatter the surrounding bit of hip. When they showed me the x-ray I almost fainted. It was deemed I would have to undergo a complete hip replacement and, as it was Friday, the appropriate surgeon was off duty and wouldn't be back until the following Monday. I only spent three nights and two days in there but it was three nights and two days of sheer agony. Dave and his wife Jackie came to visit, Yvonne sat at the side of my bed as long as visiting time would allow and the members of Northern Riots that lived in Leeds came to visit. At night I was kept sane by Audials on my mobile phone where I listened to Terry Pratchett and Rumpole of the Bailey novels. There was also an amazing night nurse that held my hand in the night when the pain got worse. It was soon discovered that I was a poet and had this book with me, (the first edition). The nurse read the Happiness poem and borrowed the book. Within a day the poem had been photocopied and was on just about every nurses station in the L.G.I. It must have been read by the nurse that came around to dispense the drugs as it earned me extra morphine.

   After the weekend I was wheeled down for the hip replacement operation and woke up back in the ward. I leant back and was just about to go to sleep when the physiotherapy team arrived. My God what a bunch of shiny happy people they are. They must go through a special "cheerful, happy, clappy chappie" series of medical training. Despite my protestations, the day after my operation they had me exercising and after two days I was walking up and down the ward with the aid of a walking frame.

      As officially I lived alone I was not allowed to go home. Instead it was agreed that I would be shipped off to my daughters house in Stamford Bridge where she and her partner Richard very kindly looked after me for a couple of months until the physios declared it was safe for me to go home.

   Once there I was hobbling around on a walking stick, Julia had looked after the cats, and I tried to pick up where I'd left off . I even managed to do one open mic spot at the Merchant, then the first Covid lockdown happened. No more gigs.

   Thanks to a couple of kind neighbours who took me for walks around Scarborough Old Town I managed to keep walking and got some fresh air. Despite the fact she was never tested we are convinced that when I was at my daughters Yvonne caught Covid and is still suffering from Long Covid. Apart from Facetime we didn't see each other for almost a year. A year in which the ex-wife continued screaming about the house, even going to the extent of attempting to sue me for non-maintenance. That silliness soon stopped when I pointed out that up to the pervious January, in addition to myself, she had been half responsible. Despite and throughout the period of Covid, estate agents were allowed to show people around houses, and I had a few viewers. Eventually an offer was made just as we went into a second period of lockdown.

Meanwhile throughout Covid I continued writing. I signed up to a website called Upwork where I pitched for a wide variety of writing jobs, and over the next two to three years I was kept busy writing a series of corporate scripts and dialogue and backgrounds for computer games. I still am.

As to the poetry, I upgraded my own tech knowledge and computer skills and began to record my poetry on my own You Tube channel where I've recorded myself reading just about everything I've ever written. I also took part in many Zoom based poetry open mics and my work was seen and heard by people all over the country, and beyond. The biggest one was a Zoom gig staged by "We Shall Overcome" that lasted the best part of a day and featured one Billy Bragg as the top of the bill. I think it was seen by twenty three thousand viewers!

I finished the eighth and ninth Agnes novels, and published two more books of my poetry. Collections Volume Two and Collections Volume Three.
 Just for the record here's a couple written during the Covid period. The first has made it into my live act.

The Devils Rock & Roll
If you lose your woman
And you lose your soul
It don't mean a damn
It's just the devils rock and roll
If your winning lottery ticket
Get's washed in your old jeans

And the bosses lay you off
Cos they've brought in a machine
And everything you touch
Seems to turn to shite
Your days are numbered
And you don't sleep well at night
Turn to the bottle to have a little tipple
When you realise your partner
Has got that extra nipple
And your credit cards been nicked
and your pockets just been picked
that your cats got hooves
and it's worked out all your moves
there's a goat inside your wardrobe
and a succubus wears your bathrobe
and there's horns on the head
of the pizza delivery man
and you realise that Black Sabbath
isn't just a band
and you went to the crossroads
but you still can't play guitar
and although the tunes been lifted
you'll always bear the scar
And God proclaimed two Richards
To us he would bequeath
Jesus gave us Cliff, but the Devil gave us Keith
and there ain't a cobbler that can
 fix the hole that's in your soul…
relax, sit back, and suck it up
It's just the devils rock and roll.
Graham Rhodes

The House in the Woods.

The house
in the woods
that nobody knows
that nobody sees
except those
that know it's there.
And they are
the very people
you never, ever
want to meet
in or out
of the woods.
Graham Rhodes

As to the move to Leeds? Well it didn't happen. Due to the state of my hip and Covid restrictions it wasn't possible to travel to Leeds to do any viewings. Also I decided that I would miss all my Scarborough friends, my gallery and most of all the sea. There's something special about living by the sea. It affects you. Despite being born in Leeds and living in London and York, these days when I'm inland I find I get a feeling of claustrophobia. It must all that space out there.

Talking of feelings, despite the fact that my hip replacement is fine I still have to use a walking stick as I seem to have lost my sense of balance. Every so often I feel like I'm falling over to my right. It's not a nice feeling. It's like suffering from vertigo. Hence for most journeys I need to get a cab everywhere.

I eventually sold the house in the old town and bought another further up in the town near to the cricket ground. Organising viewings, solicitors, and a moving van in the middle of a pandemic was a lesson in organisation. Looking back I think the D-Day landings were easier to organise.

So here I am in my new house. I miss the sea view but as its three stories I have two top rooms where one is my art studio and the second is where my books are and where I do all my writing. All in all things have worked out alright. Considering heart attacks and broken hips it could have been a hell of a lot worse. And I'm back to gigging again. Recently I did my thing again when The Northern Riots decided to call it a day and staged a farewell gig at Indigo Alley. The bill included The Fuzz Junkies, Steve Wood and the Hoods, Mr Jim and Friends and finally the Northern Riots. It was a packed, steamy night and I screamed my stuff out between the acts. It worked. Despite being 72 the young audience dug what I had to say and cheered my words. Then the following week, I was on stage again at a Jesse Hutchinson (now calling himself Caine), leaving Scarborough gig. Once again the (older) audience dug what I had to say and gave me a great reception. At both gigs it was great meeting and seeing people I hadn't seen since the lockdown. It reminded me that I made the right decision. I'm back in the gallery again, however the Council have decided to change the building into a restaurant as part of the West Pier development Plan so we'll see what happens with it. However despite the Council, I've come to realise that Scarborough is where I live and where I belong.

When I'm Gone.

When I'm gone
don't look for me
under the Yew.
Beyond stone walls,
among the weeds
and dead flowers.

Instead look for me
In the bars.
Among the smokers
at the back door,
where the music
can be heard.
Where there's
a pint to be drunk.

Graham Rhodes

END.

ACKNOWLEDGEMENTS

I would like to thank everyone who I have mentioned in this book for the part they have played in my story. It has been an absolute pleasure knowing and working with all of you. I would also like to thank the following people for their help and encouragement in getting the words down and getting the final book to print – Dave & Jackie Pruckner, Samantha and Richard, Tubbs & Missy, Julia Wray and Yvonne.

FAREWELLS AND RIP'S
Stuart Pearson
Ian Pearson
Ned Smith
Graham Cardy
Pete Cosker
Paul Garrett
Nick Jones
Jane Southam
Fang (Mark Rolf)
Mike Hurrey
Dave Codling
Baz Hampshire
Ysanne
Liam Davison
Ed
Jerry Scott
Lynda Greenwood
Tony Mallet
Aldo (Dave Alderson)

ABOUT THE AUTHOR

Graham Rhodes has over 40 years experience in writing scripts, plays, books, articles, and creative outlines. He has created concepts and scripts for broadcast television, audio-visual presentations, computer games, film & video productions, web sites, audio-tape, interactive laser-disc, CD-ROM, animations, conferences, multi-media presentations and theatres. He has created specialised scripts for major corporate clients such as Coca Cola, British Aerospace, British Rail, The Co-operative Bank, Bass, Yorkshire Water, York City Council, Provident Finance, Yorkshire Forward, among many others. His knowledge of history helped in the creation of heritage based programs seen in museums and visitor centres throughout the country. They include The Merseyside Museum, The Jorvik Viking Centre, The Scottish Museum of Antiquities, & The Bar Convent Museum of Church History.

He also wrote the scripts for two broadcast television documentaries, a Yorkshire Television religious series and a Beatrix potter Documentary for Chameleon Films and has written three film scripts, all currently looking for an interested party.

The Rebel Buccaneer,
William and Harold 1066,
Rescue (A story of the Whitby Lifeboat)

His stage plays have been performed in small venues and pubs throughout Yorkshire. "Rambling Boy" was staged at Newcastle's Live Theatre in 2003, starring Newcastle musician Martin Stephenson, whilst "Chasing the Hard-Backed, Black

Beetle" won the best drama award at the Northern Stage of the All England Theatre Festival and was performed at the Ilkley Literature Festival. Other work has received staged readings at The West Yorkshire Playhouse, been short listed at the Drama Association of Wales, and at the Liverpool Lesbian and Gay Film Festival.

He also wrote dialogue and story lines for THQ, one of America's biggest games companies, for "X-Beyond the Frontier" and "Yager" both winners of European Game of the Year Awards, and wrote the dialogue for Alan Hanson's Football Game (published by Codemasters) among many others.

OTHER BOOKS BY GRAHAM RHODES

"Footprints in the Mud of Time, The Alternative Story of York"

"The Collected Poems 1972 - 2016"

"The Collected Poems Volume 2 2016 – 2020"

"The Collected Poems Volume 3 2020-2022"

"The York Sketch Book." (a book of drawings)

"The Jazz Detective."

"Orca's Teeth" (A comedic Sci-Fi novel)

"The View from the Pink Monster"

The Agnes the Scarborough Witch Series

"A Witch, Her Cat and A Pirate."

"A Witch, Her Cat and the Ship Wreckers."

"A Witch, Her Cat and The Demon Dogs."

"A Witch her Cat and A Viking Hoard."

"A Witch her Cat and the Whistler."

"A Witch Her Cat and the Vampires."

"A Witch Her Cat and The Moon People."

"A Witch Her Cat and A Fire Demon."

"A Witch Her Cat and A Revolution."

Photographic Books

"A Visual History of York." (Book of photographs)

"Leeds Visible History" (A Book of Photographs)

"Harbourside - Scarborough Harbour
(A book of photographs available via Blurb)

"Lost Bicycles
(A book of photographs of deserted and lost bicycles available via Blurb)

"Trains of The North Yorkshire Moors
(A Book of photographs of the engines of the NYMR available via Blurb)

Printed in Great Britain
by Amazon

81221336R10161